The Lean

Palgrave Research Skills
Authoring a PhD
The Foundations of Research (2nd edn)
Getting to Grips with Doctoral Research
Getting Published
The Good Supervisor (2nd edn)
PhD by Published Work
The PhD Viva
Planning Your Postgraduate Research
The Lean PhD
The PhD Writing Handbook
The Postgraduate Research Handbook (2nd edn)
The Professional Doctorate
Structuring Your Research Thesis

Palgrave Teaching and Learning
Series Editor: Sally Brown

Access to Higher Education
Coaching and Mentoring in Higher Education
Facilitating Work-Based Learning
Facilitating Workshops
For the Love of Learning
Fostering Self-Efficacy in Higher Education Students
Internationalization and Diversity in Higher Education
Leading Dynamic Seminars
Learning, Teaching and Assessment in Higher Education
Learning with the Labyrinth
Live Online Learning
Masters Level Teaching, Learning and Assessment
Reimagining Spaces for Learning in Higher Education
Successful University Teaching in Times of Diversity

The Lean PhD

Radically Improve the Efficiency, Quality and Impact of Your Research

Julian Kirchherr

First published 2018 by
PALGRAVE

Palgrave in the UK is an imprint of Macmillan Publishers Limited, registered in England, company number 785998, of 4 Crinan Street, London N1 9XW.

Palgrave® and Macmillan® are registered trademarks in the United States, the United Kingdom, Europe and other countries.

ISBN 978–1–352–00282–9 paperback

This book is printed on paper suitable for recycling and made from fully managed and sustained forest sources. Logging, pulping and manufacturing processes are expected to conform to the environmental regulations of the country of origin.

A catalogue record for this book is available from the British Library.

A catalog record for this book is available from the Library of Congress.

To Sarah

Contents

List of Illustrative Material

Introduction

Pursuing a PhD is a major undertaking. Most universities in Europe claim that completing one will take three to four years.[1] For instance, a German PhD is supposed to take three years.[2] Meanwhile, a PhD in the United States should take five to six years.[3] However, most students do not manage to adhere to these timelines. A PhD student in Germany needs 4.6 years of full-time work on average to finish her or his PhD.[2] Those who pursue a PhD in the United States take 8.2 years of full-time work on average to complete it, according to one survey. In education sciences in the United States, a PhD can take 13 years.[4]

Despite this considerable time investment, the impact of many completed PhDs is indiscernible at best. Citations are usually seen as the main proxy for academic impact.[5] A friend of mine recently found that her PhD thesis (completed in 2008 as a traditional thesis with no papers published out of it) has not been cited a single time, according to Google Scholar. Furthermore, she found that it had only been downloaded 14 times from the respective university repository. 'And half of these downloads were probably by me,' she says. Like 40 per cent of those who completed a doctorate,[6] she is now working in a job that has nothing to do with her PhD or research in general, and comments: 'I would have been further in my corporate career if I had not done this PhD.'

It is questionable that a PhD is a reasonable time investment if it takes more than five years to complete, but is barely noticed by anyone, while not contributing to your career. This book is about turning these PhDs into endeavours that are value-adding for the student pursuing them, and beyond. It aims to explain how to radically improve the efficiency, quality and impact of your research. Its ambition is to fundamentally challenge how PhDs are currently pursued as well as the way we work in contemporary academia. There are so many insights out there these days about how to organize work efficiently and effectively. Sadly, most of these are not widely applied in the academy.

I developed the idea to write this book upon having read *Authoring a PhD: How to Plan, Draft, Write, and Finish a Doctoral Thesis or Dissertation*, written by Patrick Dunleavy who was one of my professors at the London School of Economics (LSE).[7] I also skimmed through a few comparable books prior to starting my doctorate, such as *Writing the Winning Thesis or Dissertation: A Step-by-Step Guide* by Allan Glatthorn and Randy Joyner, *Mapping Your Thesis. The Comprehensive Manual of Theory and Techniques for Masters and Doctoral Research*, by Barry White, *The Routledge Doctoral Student Companion: Getting to Grips with Research in Education and the Social Sciences*, edited by Pat Thomson and Melanie Walker, *Tricks of the Trade: How to Think about Your Research While You're Doing It*, by Howard S. Becker, *Learn to Write Badly: How to Succeed in the Social Sciences* by Michael Billig, and *How To Write a Thesis* by Rowena Murray.[8-13]

These books all contained helpful bits and pieces on how to go about a PhD. However, I found that they largely focus on the technical and stylistic aspects of the PhD endeavour (I subsume these as 'technicalities' from now on), e.g. helpful citation software to use, ways to present data, ideal length of a paragraph or chapter, typical paper or chapter structures, and different approaches to writing headings and subheadings. For instance, Dunleavy devotes one sub-chapter in his book to principles for presenting data well, while another sub-chapter is dedicated to how to devise headings and even subheadings.[7] Undoubtedly, information on these technicalities is essential for mastering a PhD and I thus recommend to readers who are unfamiliar with these points to read at least one of these books.

In my case, I felt that I already knew most of the technicalities. After all, many of them, for example how to present data well or typical paper structures, are already taught at the Bachelor's and Master's level. Meanwhile, I was seeking a more comprehensive take: how to organize the entire process of completing a PhD. Yet I did not find this process perspective outlined in any of the books I examined. This book aims to fill this perceived gap. It is not about the technicalities of a PhD. Rather, its ambition is to explain how to best organize the entire PhD process – from the very beginning to the very end.

I hope that this book is read by those who are about to embark on a PhD. This book will help you to complete your doctorate much more efficiently than you would have done otherwise, while maximizing the quality and impact that you aim to deliver. However, the ideas presented in it will also aid those who are in the midst of their PhD and those who are about to submit their thesis. Even if you have already submitted your dissertation and are now preparing for your defence, this book may still be worth a read. I also urge PhD supervisors to read this book. After all, the supervisor is a central player in implementing the PhD approach I outline. Indeed, in Chapter 5 of this book I show that many of the working principles outlined are relevant for anyone in the academy – including those who are currently writing their Bachelor's or Master's thesis.

The approach that I describe in this book is not a mere thought-construct. Rather, I tried and tested it in my PhD journey. I enrolled in my PhD programme at the School of Geography and the Environment (SOGE) at the University of Oxford in January 2015. SOGE is the world's leading school for geography.[14] I had published six peer-reviewed papers 20 months after enrolling in my PhD. Some of these were published in the world's leading journals in my field such as *Global Environmental Change, Energy Policy* and *Environmental Impact Assessment Review.* I submitted my PhD (a paper-based PhD, which meant that it consisted of a number of papers plus an introduction and conclusion) 21 months after enrolment. The average time until submission at this school is 3.8 years, according to my estimate. I was appointed as a tenure-track assistant professor at the Copernicus Institute of Sustainable Development (CISD) at Utrecht University, the Netherlands, 22 months after starting my PhD. CISD at Utrecht University is ranked as one of the world's leading research institutes on sustainable development, outpacing both Stanford University and Harvard University.[15]

My completion time was not a coincidence. Rather, it was grounded in a specific approach which I encountered while working in the private sector. This approach revolves around lean methodologies, which I define in detail in Section 1.2. I started learning about these lean methodologies while running a (not particularly successful) early stage start-up in London and Singapore back in 2012 and 2013. I further worked with lean methodologies while at a consultancy firm as a management consultant and project manager from 2013 onwards. This firm was organized around a variety of lean principles, while also offering advice to clients on how to implement these principles.

Lean methodologies are particularly hyped in the start-up community these days; among the entrepreneurs adhering to them, Eric Ries's book *The Lean Startup* has become a bible.[16] However, the core ideas (and also some of the terminology) have been around and implemented for decades by companies worldwide.[17] Examples of large corporations embracing lean principles are firms such as *AT&T*, the world's largest telecommunications company,[18] *Nokia Siemens Networks*, a major data networking player, and *The Washington Post*, a prestigious newspaper.[19] Even governments in the most remote parts of the world work along these principles nowadays. I was admitted to my PhD when I was working on a management consultancy project for an Asian provincial government where our team deployed lean methodologies to help it shape and start executing its next five-year development plan. This regional government is now experiencing tremendous success – as do so many other organizations that apply these principles. This is what motivated me to try out lean methodologies in the academy.

The approach outlined in this book is applicable across the social and natural sciences. I have successfully tried and tested its principles in geography, and my doctoral research also forged into political science, public policy, sociology and anthropology. Many PhD students from other social science disciplines as well as the arts and humanities have read drafts of this book, and some in its pages share how the proposed approach is also applicable in their disciplines. Also, PhD students from the natural sciences have read this book and some argue in it that there is no reason not to apply these working principles in the natural sciences. Yet it is true that not all advice applies equally across all disciplines. Whenever this is the case, I specifically outline this.

Each of this book's chapters draws a pointed picture of the current state of the academy. I may thus be accused of employing straw man arguments to advocate for lean principles in academia. Indeed, this picture can seem unfair to some academics, since selected academic systems have already implemented ideas proposed in this book. For instance, one reviewer noted that 'some of the points raised in this book are already quite firmly established in Australia'. Yet I chose to draw such a pointed picture of the academy to make the core ideas of this book as clear as possible, while also hoping to provoke a debate on how we currently pursue the PhD. It is thus meant as a stylistic device. Consequently, I hope that those who already implement (some of) the ideas outlined in this book may view it as a confirmation of their approaches instead of unfair criticism.

With this book being grounded in the story of my PhD, I admit that I was fortunate along the way. For instance, I was lucky with my supervisors who did not torpedo my way of working, but rather embraced it; with gaining access to numerous interviewees, which helped me to develop a unique dataset which, in turn, facilitated peer-reviewed publications; and that the niche topic that I had chosen for my PhD was of interest to prestigious academic outlets. Those who choose to embrace the approach I outline may be less lucky than I was – and/or stuck in a scholarly field where some of the ideas I outline cannot be or can only be partly implemented. However, even if you can only implement some of the ideas I outline, this may still boost the efficiency, quality and impact of your work. Some readers may be even luckier than I was, completing their PhD even more efficiently while achieving considerable quality and impact. I am keen to hear from all of you. Do reach out and share your thoughts with me regarding the ideas outlined in this book and let me know how these may have shaped your PhD journey. I will incorporate your feedback into the next edition of this book.

I could not have completed this endeavour without the constant encouragement of and feedback from my partner Sarah Tiba, the excellent feedback on the proposal and/or the full manuscript of this book by Julius Wersig, Claudia Regler and Helen Caunce, four anonymous reviewers from Palgrave and those PhD students who provided feedback on the early core ideas of this book in Gummersbach, Germany and Trondheim, Norway. I remain grateful for their contributions to this work.

JULIAN KIRCHHERR

1 The PhD as a Start-up

This chapter explains:

- Why your PhD is a start-up
- Which lean principles are most relevant to your PhD start-up
- How to manage your energy instead of your time

▶ 1.1 The PhD as a start-up

There is no definition of the term 'start-up' that any two entrepreneurs or investors agree on. Most would likely concede, though, that start-ups are firms that are (relatively) young which attempt to set something in motion.[20] Start-ups are increasingly popular among university graduates. Twenty-eight per cent of graduates from the Master of Business Administration (MBA) programme at the Stanford Graduate School of Business now seek jobs in start-ups, up from less than 20 per cent five years ago. Only traditional banks remain more popular, with 31 per cent of graduates choosing them for their further professional development.[21] Meanwhile, in a recent piece for *MarketWatch*, journalist Catey Hill lists 'academic' among the '5 once-prestigious jobs that are now B-list'[22] as fewer and fewer top talents are drawn into this sector.

However, while seemingly disparate from a perfunctory first sight, the PhD student (in the dusty world of academia) and the start-up entrepreneur (in the shiny offices of Silicon Valley) share many commonalities, as also pointed out by academic Patrick Dunleavy.[23]

First, both the start-up entrepreneur and the PhD student launch endeavours that usually commence as one-man/one-woman shows, i.e. where the one running it is, at root, alone. Much has been written about loneliness among entrepreneurs in recent years. For instance, Jonathan Hefter, the founder of Neverware, a start-up that provides software to make old computers run like new ones, shared in a *Business Insider* feature that 'starting Neverware [...] was the most isolating experience of my life'.[24] Another feature, published by *tech.co*, hypothesized that being a start-up founder may be 'the loneliest job in the world'.[25] Meanwhile, Dunleavy writes that 'researchers are always, at root, alone'.[23] Doctoral education in the United Kingdom, in particular, embraces independent and self-directed study,[26] which can isolate the one pursuing it. Half of all PhD students report suffering from psychological distress these days.[27]

Second, both the start-up entrepreneur and the PhD student must create something novel from scratch to succeed. The start-up entrepreneur needs to create an original business model that is able to disrupt and eventually outcompete the incumbents in the start-up's target industry.[28] Meanwhile, the most essential requirement for successfully completing a PhD is 'the discovery of new knowledge',[29] as the website of the University of Cambridge outlines. Similarly, the University of Warwick, also in the United Kingdom, states that 'a thesis must constitute a substantial original contribution to knowledge'.[30] If the start-up only copies and pastes existing business models, it is unlikely to survive; the first-mover advantages of the incumbents will wipe it out in most instances. Similarly, the PhD student that does not create something novel during their PhD journey is certain to fail at any serious university.

Third, both the start-up entrepreneur and the PhD student can only draw upon limited resources for their endeavours. Indeed, there are multiple start-ups that are only funded at first by bootstrapping – with the initial budget taken from the founders' limited savings and, possibly, their family and close friends. For instance, the start-up Litmus, which provides email designs and marketing tools, was launched in 2005 with only USD 800 chipped in by its three founders. The firm now has annual revenues of more than USD 6 million.[31,32] Meanwhile, many PhD students live close to or below the poverty line, as defined by their respective governments. For instance, one report found that between 15 and 20 per cent of PhD students in the social sciences and history in Germany live off less than USD 1,000 per month; the poverty line in Germany is at about USD 1,200 per month.[33] Life as an (early) start-up or PhD student can be about (financial) rags instead of riches.[34]

Fourth, both the start-up entrepreneur and the PhD student face tremendous uncertainties. After all, both endeavours revolve around developing and executing novel ideas. These new ideas – by definition – are always a journey into the unknown[35] and are thus high-risk. The PhD may be a bit less risky than the start-up, though. Sixty per cent of traditional start-ups go bust,[36–38] while roughly 50 per cent of PhD students in the United States drop out, compared to 30 per cent in the United Kingdom.[39,40] However, both the entrepreneur and the PhD student are frequently required to hide the messy aspects of their journey that result from this uncertainty, possibly creating additional pressures.[41] The venture capitalist demands a polished presentation to invest in a start-up, whereas, in the main, the professor does not want a PhD student that seems lost in the literature or data.

Fifth, there is one certainty that both the start-up entrepreneur and the PhD student share: there is a thorny journey ahead of them. Those running Dreamit, a start-up accelerator, write that 'even founders who have multi-million dollar exits to their names [...] face constant rejection with their current ventures'.[42] After all, initially, only a few understand the novel idea pursued by the company. Otherwise the firm would have been founded a long time ago. Many PhD students can identify with this. Harsh criticism of their work by their supervisor(s) and assessors is the norm, and with more papers churned out than ever before[43] even B-journals (which are acceptable, but not particularly renowned) reject most papers submitted to them these days. For instance, one B-journal in my field rejects almost 70 per cent of all papers submitted to it.[44] Meanwhile, more than 92 per cent of all submissions to *Nature* are rejected.[45]

Start-up entrepreneurs and PhD students both launch as one-person shows. Both must create something novel from scratch with limited resources. Both face an uncertain journey ahead of them with the only certainty being many obstacles along the way. Hence, the start-up and the PhD are remarkably similar undertakings. However, the success of an academic often seems a result of individual determination or mere luck, while successful start-ups increasingly share the same set of underlying principles. Indeed, some of those founding a start-up have developed a set of working principles in the past which help them to launch firms that become almost instantly successful. For instance, it took Dropbox seven months to get its first million users.[46] Meanwhile, Spotify hit its first million users only five months after its launch,[47] Instagram after only 2.5 months.[48] Given the various commonalities between start-up entrepreneurs and PhD students, PhD students may be able to learn much from the working principles of start-ups.

▶ 1.2 Going lean

Start-ups come in all shapes and sizes. However, many now share a common underpinning: the lean start-up approach. Successful start-ups such as those we have already mentioned – Dropbox, Spotify and Instagram – as well as start-ups such as Wealthfront, an algorithm that manages your stock investments, or Aardvark, a social search engine recently acquired by Google, have built their businesses with lean methodologies.[49-51] And the dominance of lean methodologies continues to grow with organizations like Start-up Weekend now expanding to almost every larger city around the world. Start-up Weekend runs 54-hour events that create a business model prototype within this timeframe. The entire event is centred around the lean start-up approach, thus introducing hundreds of prospective entrepreneurs at a time to these principles.[37] Also, more than 25 universities around the world now teach lean methodologies to the next generation of entrepreneurs and an online programme on lean working principles is one of the most popular at Udacity, a start-up offering massive open online courses

(MOOCs),[37] which itself deploys lean working principles for its growth.[52] Indeed, there are only a few left in the start-up landscape that have not been influenced by the lean start-up approach.

The term 'lean start-up' was coined by entrepreneur Eric Ries in a blogpost in 2008.[53] It went mainstream after the publication of his 2011 book *The Lean Startup* which sold 100,000 copies,[54,55] and it was further popularized by the 2012 book *The Startup Owner's Manual* by the entrepreneur and academic Steve Blank and entrepreneur Bob Dorf.[56] Whereas the lean start-up approach is mostly grounded in Ries's book, the term gained so much momentum that a variety of users embraced it and amended it once it was applied. Thus, the term is now a buzzword that means many different things to different people – keeping Ries busy posting articles which attempt to further clarify his interpretation of the term.[57] This book is not attempting to comprehensively apply the lean start-up approach outlined by Ries. Rather, I took (my interpretation of) those ideas from Ries that I found most relevant to the academic context and then modified them, at times significantly, to suit it.

The three main ideas from the lean start-up approach particularly embraced in this book are the concept of a minimum viable product, rapid prototyping and end-user orientation:

- *Minimum viable product.* Academicians are infamous for their perfectionism, with the website *insidehighered.com* even devoting an entire subsection to this topic.[58] With many at the top of the academic ladder embracing perfectionism, more and more generations of perfectionist academicians are nurtured.[59] Meanwhile, those who advocate the concept of a minimum viable product (MVP) are fundamentally at odds with perfectionism. MVP adherents want to build a product that is not perfect, but 'good enough'. This means that the product needs to entail its envisaged core features, but nothing else. (This already indicates that the paper route is the preferred format for the PhD approach I outline in this book; I further discuss this in Section 2.5.) MVP adherents attempt to build the MVP as fast as possible while deploying as few resources as possible.[16]
- *Rapid prototyping.* However, the ambition of those embracing the MVP concept is still to deliver a perfect product, and rapid prototyping is chosen as a means for achieving this. Rapid prototyping means that the MVP is exposed to its potential end users once completed, feedback is then collected from these users, the MVP is amended according to this feedback and it is then exposed again to the end users for additional feedback. Ries calls this a 'build-measure-learn' loop which continues until the end users wholeheartedly embrace the product developed. Again, this approach is at odds with the academy since its perfectionists are conditioned to only share their products – which can be a

presentation for a conference, an academic paper or a thesis – with their peers (their primary end users) once these products are as polished as possible.

- *End-user orientation.* The MVP is *what* the lean start-up adherent produces first; rapid prototyping is *how* they improve it. The end user is *why* the lean start-up adherent undertakes this effort. Every action of the lean start-up proponent is orientated towards the end user. The difference between this end-user orientation of the lean start-up proponent and the orientation of the traditional academic can be stark, at least in some disciplines. Although grant funders increasingly pressure scholars to produce work with a societal end user in mind, with societal impact of scholarly work thus becoming more and more relevant, discussing end-user orientation of research can still be frowned upon within the academy, according to my experience.[35] 'Academics do not work for the end users, but for the sake of the academy', a professor at Oxford University recently told me.

An example to illustrate the three principles outlined above: Nick Swinmurn, an entrepreneur in the United States, wanted to launch a company in the late 1990s that would sell shoes online, a seemingly mundane undertaking nowadays. If Swinmurn had been an academic, he would have developed a polished website for many months (or possibly even more than a year), coupled with the setting up of a complex storage facility as his firm's back-end that would comprise a selection of his favourite shoes. He would have spent tens of thousands of dollars prior to even knowing if anyone wanted to buy his favourite shoes online. This is not what Swinmurn did.

Instead, Swinmurn went to several local shoe stores, took pictures of their inventory and posted them on one of his existing websites. This was his MVP. When people started ordering shoes from his offering, he went to the stores where he had taken the photos, bought the shoes ordered at the retail price and sent them to his customers. Prior to launching this MVP, an MVP with no dedicated front-end and no back-end whatsoever, Swinmurn had been unsure if his envisaged end users were willing to buy shoes online. His MVP allowed him to quickly and cost-efficiently test this. The company founded out of this MVP was Zappos which sold for more than one billion USD to Amazon in 2009.[16,60]

Admittedly, Swinmurn the academic may still have been successful with his business idea since the core idea proved to be sound. Nonetheless, the lean Swinmurn would have been able to launch the business much faster – and this first-mover advantage cannot be underestimated in any sector. At the time of the business launch for academic Swinmurn, the lean Swinmurn would have already run a functioning business with many customers. It would have been very difficult for academic Swinmurn to catch up.

There are at least three consequences for those who apply the lean principles in the academy and this story hints at them: greater efficiency, greater quality and greater impact. The level of efficiency is indicated by the time needed from starting to develop a product such as a PhD until it is satisfactory to its end users. Adopting the principles outlined above ensures that from the very beginning of the PhD much scholarly input is gathered to tailor it to the scholarly community – considered the end user for the PhD – while as little time as possible is wasted by running into dead ends. Meanwhile, the student that embraces traditional scholarly working principles risks that months and months (and sometimes even years) of work will be judged as inadequate once shared with the scholarly community. In this case, the student would have to start again from square one and would lose a great deal of time. Eventually, funding for the PhD would run out and the student may be unable to submit.

Defining efficiency in this way highlights its inherent quality. If a PhD of substandard quality is submitted, it will fail. Hence, it will not be an efficient PhD. Furthermore, quality is (at least in theory) a precondition of impact. It is thus at the very heart of the lean PhD approach. Indeed, the lean PhD is all about radically improving the quality of your research. The result of this is impact: the take-up of a product by its end users. Most within academia distinguish between academic and societal impact. Academic impact is usually measured by the number of citations, as outlined previously. The more feedback that is collected and incorporated from scholars, the higher the quality of the PhD for the relevant community and the greater its visibility. Hence, the higher the likelihood that the work will be cited by colleagues.

Admittedly, citations are an imperfect proxy for academic impact. First, self-citations can boost one's citation count just as much as citation by colleagues, without indicating any true impact on the field. Some academics justify self-citations by joking that you can never truly cite others until you have learnt to cite yourself. Tellingly, men cite their own papers 56 per cent more than women on average, according to a recent analysis.[61] Second, even citations of your work by colleagues may not indicate scholarly impact. For instance, imagine a citation that reads: 'Scholar A has also written on this topic, as have scholars B, C and D.' It would count just as much as a citation that reads: 'I build my paper on the method developed by scholar A.' While the latter citation indicates impact on the field, the former does not. Nevertheless, the citation count rises just as much with the former type of citation as it does with the latter.

Meanwhile, a citation that reads 'scholar A falsely argues that...' is one that many scholars would like to pass on, but it still also boosts the citation count.[62] However, some scholars may not mind this kind of citation, which indicates some degree of controversy. Indeed, controversy in papers can vastly boost the citation count. A recent example of this is a paper with the provocative title 'In Defense of Colonialism' by Bruce Gilley, an associate professor of political science at Portland State University. This piece was published in *Third World*

Quarterly, a respected development journal.[63] It achieved the highest Altmetric score, a measure for a paper's social media influence that is also seen as an indicator of its future academic impact, of any paper ever published in the journal.[64] (The paper was eventually retracted because the editor of *Third World Quarterly* received credible threats of violence due to its publication.[65])

Discussions abound these days regarding the necessity to also create practical impact with scholarly work. Evidently, practitioners will only integrate such works into their thinking and, ultimately, their conduct if their quality is appreciated. While many supervisors may find that there is not enough time within a PhD to also start chasing practical impact, more and more recruiters (including academic recruiters) want to know about a PhD's societal impact.[66] This impact, for example on attitudes or policies, is more difficult to measure than academic impact and it is particularly difficult in disciplines such as English literature or theology. Any PhD student is well-advised to start thinking about it early. I outline how to specifically maximize the practical impact of a PhD in Section 4.5.

▶ 1.3 Managing your energy

The approach outlined in this book can significantly increase the efficiency of the PhD endeavour, while boosting its quality and impact. Nevertheless, the proposed lean PhD is still one that requires ample effort and time. A lean PhD is not a cheap one. Entrepreneur Lee Hower writes that any start-up (including the lean one) requires someone 'fundamentally committed to putting in all the blood, sweat and tears'[67] that are needed to get a company off the ground. This is echoed by, inter alios, Marissa Mayer, former Chief Executive Officer of Yahoo, who argues:

> [I]f you go into a co-working space on a Saturday afternoon, I can tell you which start-ups will succeed, without even knowing what they do. Being there on the weekend is a huge indicator of success, mostly because these companies don't just happen. They happen because of really hard work.[68]

She believes that the secret to success is working 130 hours a week.[69]

This book does not propagate that you work 130 hours a week to complete your PhD. It also does not promise that you will complete your PhD by adopting the four-hour working week.[70] Any PhD will always require many hours. However, the lean PhD will significantly reduce the hours needed. I estimate that it may halve it, given that I submitted my PhD in 45 per cent of the average time needed until submission at my school, as I outlined at the beginning of this book. The lean PhD approach may even save more time for those who are particularly inclined to adopt the traditional approach to academia. It allows you to work more efficiently (and thus less intensely), while improving the quality and impact of your endeavour.

No PhD, though, requires putting in a certain number of hours until it is completed, although some students seem to think this. They are then surprised if they make little progress even though they invest 60 hours or more per week into their work. Start-up entrepreneurs also frequently boast about the time they put in, and still go bust. Those who count their hours may be better off focusing on their energy. Indeed, much empirical research indicates that productivity has less to do with the amount of hours we invest in a single working day, and more with the rest we have.[71,72] This may be a particularly encouraging finding for those who undertake a part-time PhD by choice or necessity. If the slots allocated to work on the PhD are slots where one is energized (and thus does not procrastinate – the average American worker wastes around 50 minutes at work every day[73]), it is still possible to progress quickly.

While I worked a lot on my PhD when I worked on it, I did not always work on it during the 21 months from start to completion. In fact, I did a lot of other things as well which energized me and thus eventually helped me to progress efficiently in my research. For instance, I wrote and published numerous op-eds throughout my PhD on topics entirely unrelated to my research (I enjoy popular writing). I also completed full-time projects with a consulting company while pursuing my PhD. And yes, I also went on vacation. When I felt that my fundamental drive for my PhD topic had dipped (which I believe inevitably happens in any PhD), I often did something else.

This guidance is not meant to suggest, though, only working on your PhD when you feel like it. There will be many days when you do not feel like working on it. After all, the road to PhD completion is a thorny one and thus not always enjoyable. I generally recommend sitting down and starting to work on your PhD even on those days when you do not feel like it. Only when you have worked on your PhD for four or five hours and not made any progress at all could it be time to do something else – if this does not become a routine. To complete the PhD, you will need to sometimes push, even if your energy is low.

I can always push most when there is a clear target that energizes me. One target in my PhD was (and I do not suggest emulating this!) to complete it in 18 months. Reminding myself of this target would help me to push myself through these days where my energy was low. A target that may work for you could be to send out that first paper, or to only go on that vacation to Honduras once that data collection is completed. While some thrive most on the grand targets, many PhD students I talk to tell me that it is the more manageable ones that can be accomplished in a few weeks or even days that boost their motivation most.

So much for initial guidance on how to pursue the lean PhD. I will now delve into how to manage the entire PhD process – from the very beginning to the very end. This journey is summarized in Figure 1.1.

Launching	Executing	Exiting
1. Fill out the lean PhD canvas	1. Embrace the minimum viable paper	1. Embrace the minimum viable dissertation
2. Choose an academic niche market	2. Write, write, write	2. Strategically choose examiners
3. Write a lean research proposal	3. Assemble a powerful paper team	3. Aim for revisions
4. Find an early career supervisor	4. Find students to work with	4. Go the extra mile
5. Embrace the paper route	5. Visit many, many conferences	5. Boost practical impact
6. Creatively secure resources	6. Consider pivoting	6. Consider exiting

Figure 1.1 The lean PhD journey

2 Launching the PhD

This chapter explains:

- How the lean PhD canvas can help structure your thinking regarding your vision for your PhD endeavour
- Why, for your PhD, topics that currently gather limited interest are to be preferred to booming topics
- How to go about writing a research proposal
- Why an early career supervisor is usually more helpful than a star professor
- Why choosing the paper route instead of writing a thesis is to be recommended
- Where to find funding for your PhD

▶ 2.1 The lean PhD canvas

A start-up entrepreneur faces countless questions when launching their endeavour. What market is best to target? How should the endeavour be framed? Who will be willing to fund it? The lean canvas is a framework that helps start-ups adhering to lean methodologies to comprehensively think through these questions.[74] In Table 2.1 you will find the lean PhD canvas. It is inspired by the lean canvas, although it has been adapted significantly to suit the academic context. There are five areas to think through when launching your PhD endeavour. First, you need to decide on the academic market you aim to target. Second, you want to consider how to approach your research proposal. Third, you need to decide on supervisors; fourth, on the format; and finally, on resourcing. Table 2.1 outlines key questions to ask for each of these areas, while the remainder of this chapter explains how to answer these if you are keen to follow the lean PhD approach.

Try this ... for getting started on your PhD

- Fill out the PhD canvas once you are fired up about pursuing a PhD
- Do not take more than 30 minutes to do this
- Share your PhD canvas with family and friends for discussion

Table 2.1 The lean PhD canvas

A. Academic Market
• Which potential PhD topics interest you?
• Which of these topics attract a lot of attention? Which are niche markets?
• Do you have an unfair advantage in any of the niche markets you are interested in?

B. Research Proposal	C. Supervision	D. Format
• Can you name three topics (one bullet point per topic) within your favourite academic market(s) that you are keen to pursue? • Who are potential stakeholders to discuss your research topic ideas with?	• What supervisors are available for your potential research topics at the most prestigious universities? • Which of these supervisors are most promising?	• Is it possible to pursue a paper-based PhD at your target university and discipline? • Is your potential supervisor supportive of the paper-based PhD?

E. Resources
• Is there potential to secure funding for your PhD via crowdsourcing?
• Which firm(s) may be keen to fund your PhD?
• What are the different governmental scholarships available in your country and beyond?
• What would a research associate position to fund your PhD entail?

▶ 2.2 Choosing an (academic) market

The lean start-up approach that I presented in Chapter 1 of this book was not specific to a market. Indeed, Eric Ries wants his readers to believe that this approach is so powerful that it helps to create a winning start-up in any market. I disagree and so do many entrepreneurs.[75] While the lean start-up approach may raise your odds of being successful in any market, the chosen market itself may be the most essential determinant for a start-up's success or failure. 'Market matters most' many tell you in Silicon Valley. If the start-up entrepreneur operates in a great market – a market with many customers, one that is growing and one with limited competition – the start-up will be pulled along by it.[75]

There are also markets for PhD students. Your market is the topic you choose. If you decide to do a PhD on the circular economy, my current research topic, the various scholarly publications on this topic constitute your academic market. Similarly, if you choose sustainable business models as the focus of your PhD, the papers and books on this topic are the market that you compete in. Many PhD students I know tend to pick markets that are booming. This means they choose trending topics. One example is 'start-ups'. Everyone talks about start-ups these days (this book is no exception) so many find this topic interesting and thus want to do their PhD on it.

The most straightforward way to find out if a topic is one in a booming market is to search for recent scholarly literature reviews on it via academic search engines such as Scopus or Thomson Reuters' Web of Science. These articles may be framed as 'literature review', 'meta-analysis' or 'meta-synthesis'. Most frequently, they will depict the development of the number of articles per year for a topic at question. More than 100 articles were published on the circular economy in 2016, compared to only about 30 articles in 2014, according to one literature review.[76] Hence this is a topic that is now booming.

Try this ... for choosing an (academic) market

- Make a list of topics you find fascinating
- Note down which topics are booming topics and which ones are niches (with momentum)
- Identify topics on your list in which you have an 'unfair advantage'

A topic that is booming may fascinate you. And there is nothing wrong with choosing a topic for your PhD that you find fascinating. Indeed, I highly recommend that you only do a PhD on a topic that you are extremely excited about. After all, there will be many tedious hours ahead of you even if you follow the lean PhD approach throughout your doctoral studies, as outlined earlier. The precondition of staying the course is a genuine interest in your research topic. You will end up procrastinating endlessly if you only pick a topic that it is rational to choose – for example because you identified a fantastic supervisor in the subject who even embraces the paper route – but that does not fascinate you.

I was and remain fascinated by large dams. It is their tremendous impact that enthrals me. Large dams may be the most significant single human intervention in nature; their resulting impacts – both positive and negative – are vast.[77,78] For instance, dams have displaced up to 80 million people worldwide in the past century.[79] At the same time, large dams provide 16 per cent of all global electricity.[80] Single dams can even power entire countries. For instance, the Itaipu Dam on the border between Brazil and Paraguay supplies 26 per cent of all electrical power needed in Brazil and a staggering 78 per cent of all electrical power needed in Paraguay.[81,82] It is this potential for impact that drew me, first and foremost, to dams as my PhD topic.

There is more than one topic that interests most people, though. If the topic that you consider pursuing for your PhD is one that is trending, I urge you to reconsider. Maybe there is another topic that interests you just as much, but which is not as hyped. This could be a more sensible choice for your PhD for at least two reasons.

First, it will take much less to be admitted to an outstanding university with such a topic, and these prestigious universities matter a lot. Consider that many PhD students even at the most prestigious universities are not particularly successful researchers. A 2014 paper in the *Journal of Economic Perspectives* examined the research productivity of 14,300 scholars who received an economics PhD from 154 American and Canadian institutions. The authors measured how many papers equivalent to a paper in the *American Economic Review*, the most prestigious economics journal, were published by the PhD students over the course of their studies. Unsurprisingly, they found that PhD students from the most renowned institutions can be extremely productive. For instance, the 99th percentile from Harvard and MIT – the most productive 1 per cent of the graduating class – published more than four *American Economic Review*-equivalent papers during their PhD. However, they also found that the number of *American Economic Review*-equivalent papers of the median PhD student at Harvard and MIT is only at 0.2, whereas the top 1 per cent of students at non-prestigious universities manage to produce about as many *American Economic Review*-equivalent papers as those at Harvard and MIT.[83] 'Top researchers come from a range of institutions, not just the best ones', *The Economist* summarized.[84]

Yet it appears that the top researchers from non-prestigious academic institutions are usually not the ones that end up in academic jobs. Indeed, other research indicates that faculty hiring has little to do with performance during the PhD. A widely cited 2015 paper in *Science Advances* scrutinized more than 16,000 faculty members in the fields of business, computer science and history at 242 universities. It found that a quarter of all universities account for 71 to 86 per cent of all tenure-track faculty staff in the United States and Canada in these three fields. Just 18 elite universities produce half of all computer science professors, 16 schools produce half of all business professors, and eight schools account for half of all history professors.[85,86] Hence, this study suggests that a PhD student will face an uphill battle in securing an academic job (assuming that they actually want one) if they completed the PhD, even if it was an outstanding one, at a second-tier university.

Hence, landing a PhD offer at a prestigious university may be a core aim of the launch phase of the PhD. Yet competition for the few PhD spots on this topic at this university will be fierce. It can thus be advantageous to aim for a topic that you find interesting and that is researched at this university, but that is currently not receiving much attention since fewer students will apply for these spots. Climate change is a particularly hyped topic in geography. Those scholars working on this topic at a prestigious university can receive hundreds of applications each year, while only able to recruit two to three PhD students at a time. Meanwhile, many other scholars at the same university working on niche topics may only receive a handful of PhD applicants per year, while also hoping to recruit two to three PhD students per year. Climate scientists can be extremely picky when screening applications. This is a different story for the scholars working on niche topics – students with mediocre applications may even be admitted at times.

Scholars working on a hyped topic can also create a second issue for a PhD student then admitted to this topic: too many scholars attempting to publish on this topic. Peer-reviewed papers in leading journals signal to assessors the scholarly quality of the completed work and thus help to ensure that you pass your PhD. Most journals are keen to publish articles from a variety of topics. Hence the size of a niche topic market – which are the pages allocated in a journal for it – is not much smaller than that of a hyped topic. However, these journals will receive many more submissions on a specific hyped topic than on other topics. The editors-in-chief may respond by allocating a bit more space in the journal to this hyped topic. But the supply of articles on it will usually still surpass demand. Hence, the editors-in-chief will be rather picky regarding the articles they publish on a hyped topic in their respective outlets, whereas they may be grateful for submissions on niche topics which are crucial to feature to present a balanced volume. The hyped topic is a topic that is difficult to publish on.

Choosing a niche topic may facilitate admission to a prestigious university as well as to journal publications. Ideally, you choose a niche topic with a decent chance of becoming a booming topic soon. This would then be a great market – many potential customers, high growth and limited competition. I embraced two niche topics related to dams throughout my PhD studies: socio-economic impacts of dams and anti-dam movements. I thought that these may be topics turning from niche into growth topics during my PhD. After all, there is an unprecedented boom in dam construction underway with 3,700 dams, each with a capacity of more than 1 megawatt, either planned or under construction.[87,88] My hypothesis was that this boom would trigger scholarly interest in the topic – this hope has not entirely materialized so far.

One additional reason why I chose my topic was because I had an unfair advantage in it. An unfair advantage is one that cannot easily be copied or bought.[89] The lean canvas urges start-up founders to think about their unfair advantage from the very first day of their endeavour since the start-up's competitors will attempt to copy or buy any unique value preposition (UVP) that the founder develops, with the UVP thus vanishing rapidly. An unfair advantage can be the founder's single-minded, uncompromising obsession with a specific topic or access to (not illegal) inside information.

When I started reading on my eventual PhD research topic, I found that scholars in my academic market had barely been able to gather data from private sector players in the dam industry so far since these players would not trust most scholars (scholars in my field tend to side with non-governmental organizations (NGOs) which are the main antagonists of dam developers[90]). I hypothesized that my background in the private sector would help me to build trust with private sector players in the dam industry and that I could also leverage my former employer, a consulting firm, for relevant introductions. This turned out to be true.

However, for those hoping to pursue an academic career after their PhD, choosing a niche topic may entail some pitfalls – and I learnt this one the hard way. As I outlined earlier, I completed my PhD in a very short time and I published six papers prior to the submission of my PhD. I then had very great difficulty finding an academic job despite having graduated from a prestigious university. After all, universities are usually keen to hire scholars who work on hyped topics, not those on niche topics, since these hyped topics are the ones funding bodies release calls for proposals on, journalists are keen to report on and students want to learn about. Accordingly, niche fields have few job openings.

Once I realized that universities did not care at all about the work I had done during my PhD, I started pitching a hyped topic to them. For instance, I wrote in my application to Utrecht University that 'I intend to significantly broaden my research in the coming years. I am particularly interested in the circular economy (CE) concept'. I identified the circular economy as a suitable topic to pitch to Utrecht University since it was the only topic the research group I applied to worked on that at least my practical experiences could relate to (sadly, this does not count for very much in academia); I had never published anything on the circular economy. At the same time, it was a booming topic that the university wanted

I am currently pursuing a PhD in finance. It is quite easy in this discipline to get carried away by the glamour of the immensely reputed PhD programmes that lead those global ranking tables. The typical applicant will pitch to these programmes that they would write the PhD on one of the currently booming topics in finance. However, identifying a niche market may well help an aspirant more. I also went for one of the booming topics in finance these days, the dynamics of algorithmic trading and how this impacts order books and market microstructure. With the benefit of hindsight, I find that my topic choice may have been a mistake. While I managed to be admitted to a highly prestigious programme, I now wonder how I will differentiate in the market later on with my booming topic. Indeed, that differentiation is much easier if you consciously searched for and chose a niche topic. I also see now how it is much easier to publish on a niche topic in prestigious journals, as compared to a booming topic for which that journal may receive dozens of similar submissions in a single month. If I could wind back time, I would probably now go for a topic that is receiving much less attention than my current one. Choosing a topic for your PhD is really one of the most important decisions in your PhD journey. I urge any PhD student to think about this most carefully.

Baridhi Malakar, PhD Student (Finance), Georgia Institute of Technology, United States

someone for. With my circular economy pitch, I was shortlisted and eventually landed a job offer from Utrecht University. My PhD from the University of Oxford likely also helped to overcome my lack of relevant research experience. This switch in research focus that I undertook during my job search is called 'pivoting' in the lean start-up approach. I further discuss this in Chapter 3.

▶ 2.3 The lean research proposal

Start-up entrepreneurs used to write lengthy business plans, often of 60 pages or more, before the lean start-up movement. Months and months could be spent on honing these business plans. They would frequently be backed by complex Excel models that would project the start-up's costs and revenues not only for the next year, but for the next five, 10 or even 15 years. Indeed, these business plans were the exact opposite of the minimum viable product (MVP) concept and all too often start-up entrepreneurs would realize upon finishing their business plan that they had spent many resources on developing a plan for a product that nobody wanted.[74] Business plans rarely survive contact with first customers.[37]

Many prospective PhD students are remarkably like the start-up entrepreneur prior to the lean start-up movement. A friend of mine from the consulting firm where I worked took a four-week sabbatical to write his PhD research proposal. At the end of the four weeks, he had written a 15-page research proposal. I read it and I found it interesting. He sent it out to prospective professors at the University of Oxford, his target university for the envisaged PhD. Most professors did not reply. Those who replied did not find it interesting. He never enrolled at the University of Oxford.

If my friend had adhered to lean methodologies, he would have developed an MVP of a research proposal and then collected feedback from prospective supervisors to hone it. Instead, he overwhelmed prospective supervisors with a polished proposal. The impression of the supervisors was likely that this potential student already knew exactly what he wanted to do and that thus the supervisor could not shape the research journey – a key interest of many supervisors. The thorough preparation of my friend prior to reaching out to potential supervisors was possibly detrimental to his success.

The potential supervisor is to the PhD student what the business angel is to the start-up: the first sponsor of the endeavour, needed for it to take initial shape. There are few start-ups without a business angel in their seed stage and there are no PhD students without a supervisor. Hence, the interests and perspectives of this first sponsor are most essential. They need to be gathered early on since it is difficult to impossible to guess them without first contact. The PhD supervisor is the main end user of the research proposal, the product that the PhD student develops during the launch phase. After all, the PhD supervisor in most countries around the world solely or mostly decides about the admission of the PhD student to a programme.

In Figure 2.1 I share the MVP I developed for my first Skype discussion with the person that became the first supervisor of my PhD. It is one dense and polished PowerPoint slide. Nevertheless, I essentially only sketched three very different research ideas on this slide with a few bullet points on each. In addition, I also noted down some ideas regarding methodological approaches to take – and I should have probably also thought a bit about the envisaged theoretical framing of my work. I summarize the different tasks you may undertake to prepare for the first call with your potential supervisor in Table 2.2. This is all that is needed for the first conversation with a potential supervisor.

I introduced the three research ideas from Figure 2.1 to my potential supervisor during the call and then asked which one of them she would find most interesting. She told me that she liked the first one most and I collected her input to further develop this idea. It took me maybe 45 minutes to develop this slide. Imagine if I had developed a full-fledged research proposal on the third research idea outlined

Table 2.2 'Are you prepared for the first call with your potential supervisor?' checklist

#	Question	Answer
1	Have you developed at least three core ideas for your research?	
2	Do you have initial ideas regarding methodological approaches that could be taken to research these core ideas?	
3	Do you have a first idea regarding a theoretical grounding of your proposed work?	
4	Have you read the most recent as well as the most cited articles that relate to your core research ideas?	
5	Have you read the most recent as well as the most cited articles by your potential supervisor?	

on the slide prior to the call. I could have spent four weeks on developing this proposal, only to learn that my supervisor did not find the general idea interesting enough for a PhD. I may never have pursued my PhD with her then.

Based on the input of my eventual supervisor, which reflected her deep understanding regarding possible opportunities in my envisaged field, I went on to develop my proposal. I took one week off work to research for it and write it down; I would recommend a week to any prospective PhD student as the maximum time for producing the first draft of their proposal. I only needed a quarter of the time my friend did since the call with my prospective supervisor had given me direction. Following the week of research and writing, I shared the proposal with my potential supervisor and she provided detailed feedback on it. This helped me to further hone my research questions and to add more granularity to the methods proposed. I asked her for another round of feedback, but she did not have time for it. Hence, I applied for the PhD based on two build-measure-learn loops. I was admitted to the PhD programme at the School of Geography and the Environment, University of Oxford, in May 2014.

The requirements regarding an eventual PhD proposal differ vastly from discipline to discipline and even from university to university within a specific discipline. The university websites usually offer concrete information on these requirements and I urge you to familiarize yourself with this information as early as possible – ideally even before the first call with your prospective supervisor. Oxford University's School of Geography and the Environment requires a research proposal that 'is usually around 2,500 words long although there is no upper or lower limit to this'.[91] The research proposal must include four sections: one on background and rationale of the research project, one on research

Ideas related to environmental, social and economic challenges associated with hydropower could be detailed in proposal

Overview – Initial research ideas on hydropower

Type of exploitation barrier	Possible deep dive	Details	Methodological approach
Environmental	**Environmental impact of hydropower project in Myanmar**	• Controversial (currently suspended) **Myitsone Hydroelectric Project (Myanmar)** mainly assessed from economic/social perspective – Huge environmental implications, though[1] • Quantifying environmental costs of the project	• Tailor-made environmental impact assessment (EIA) accounting for Burmese context of severely limited data availability • Methodological starting point EIA approaches in *Environmental Impact Assessment Review* (bit.ly/1hFx3BG)
Social	**Citizen attitudes towards hydropower**	• Citizen protests key barriers to many dam projects Understanding root causes of citizen skepticism, developing possible response strategies	• Focus groups, semi-structured interviews, possibly experiments[2] • Methodological example may be Fell & Chiu (2014, bit.ly/1mtYscK)
Economic	**Modernizing hydropower in Europe**	• ~70% of hydro capacity in Western Europe older than 30 years (cf. back-up) possibly leading to hydropower degeneration • Identifying root causes of modernization backlog, recommended response strategies, likelihood of implementing them[3]	• Semi-structured interviews with experts, data/document analysis • Methodological example could be Rosenow (2012, bit.ly/Kx3nur)

- Environmental impact of hydropower project in Myanmar, citizen attitudes and modernization of hydropower in Europe initial ideas for further exploration
- Open for additional/alternative suggestions – Overview only meant as starting point for discussion

1 E.g., project threatening one of the world's greatest biodiversity hot spots 2 On testing approaches to overcome citizen skepticism towards hydropower – Regional focus of project to be decided upon beforehand 3 Only in selected country/countries

SOURCE: Quoted journals & articles, World Bank; McKinsey; author's analysis

Figure 2.1 Example of the MVP of a research proposal

questions to be tackled, one on the theoretical framework and envisaged methodology and, finally, one on methods.

If you are unable to obtain any feedback from your potential supervisor prior to submitting your research proposal, this guidance on university websites can be of particular help. Furthermore, it can help you to scrawl through your potential supervisor's most recent publications (and even tweets) to tweak your proposal as much as possible to align with their work. If you have been able to obtain some feedback from your supervisor, but you feel that it is not sufficient, you may want to consider discussing the proposal with additional stakeholders. These can be your friends or family or acquaintances who are at least somewhat familiar with your proposed work. Your research proposal will become more convincing the more feedback you gather and incorporate. Any feedback is a gift.

The reader may regard my strategy of approaching the supervisor as opportunistic since it caters so much to the interests of the supervisor instead of those of the prospective student. Yet launching the lean PhD does not equate to giving up your research interests. First, the student still proposes the initial research theme in this model and this should be grounded in their interests, as discussed earlier. Second, the topic then outlined in the research proposal will not be the final topic of the PhD anyway. I already outlined in Chapter 1 that research is an uncertain and thus a highly dynamic process. Hence, the researcher barely ever ends up where they envisaged they would.

Indeed, the decisions regarding the research questions outlined in the research proposal are only loosely indicative (at most) of the research questions finally answered in the dissertation. I proposed environmental impacts of large dams as one of three topics in the initial Skype call with my eventual PhD supervisor. My submitted research proposal centred around social impacts of dams, and I was awarded a PhD for my work on anti-dam movements. While the theme of my research, dams, remained, the specific topic changed considerably, and this is normal within the research process. I thus find that prospective PhD students who develop a research proposal that is broadly connected to the theme they find interesting and that is based on the continuous feedback of their prospective supervisor and additional stakeholders are most efficient in developing their proposal.

As an assistant professor, I can now admit PhD students myself. While I initially asked these students to write a lean research proposal, I have recently even stopped asking for this. As soon as I am convinced that someone has the passion and brains needed for a PhD, all I ask them to come up with is one concrete idea for their very first paper. I then start working with them on this first paper immediately upon their admission. This paper provides the students with the insights into the field and its research gaps. Their interests will also develop while working on this first paper. We then discuss what to do for the second paper a few weeks before the first paper is submitted.

Insights from a PhD researcher

When I wanted to launch my PhD, I started out by writing down multiple research questions around three main themes that I found most interesting and that I had at least some experience with. I wrote these down on a single page only. This took me maybe two hours at most. With this lean research proposal, I then started approaching possible supervisors. All of them quickly provided feedback on my proposal and this was probably because my proposal was so compact. Via this feedback, I could then figure out which potential supervisor was most responsive to my ideas and thus most suitable. My eventual supervisor really embraced one of my outlined themes, European Union state aid law on risk capital for small- and medium-sized enterprises, and then helped me to elaborate on it. For instance, he shared with me the most relevant literature on this topic, he helped me to sharpen my proposed methodological approach and he also helped me to frame my topic in such a way that it would be relevant both for academics and practitioners. I would really recommend to anyone to go lean in the very beginning of your PhD. It will save you a lot of time, while you will still end up with a topic for your eventual PhD that combines your interests and experience.

Maximilian Vollmer, PhD Student (Law), Maastricht University, the Netherlands

▶ 2.4 Finding an early career supervisor

Start-up entrepreneurs usually chase the most prominent funders since their investment is believed to signal the start-up's quality to the market. For instance, the German start-up Scalable Capital, an algorithm that manages stock investments, now boasts everywhere that Blackrock, the world's largest asset manager, recently invested more than USD 30 million in it.[92] I outlined earlier in this chapter why it makes sense to seek supervisors at prestigious universities. There are two types of supervisors at these universities, however: star professors and those whose work is (still) largely unknown. PhD students also often seek to be supervised by the most renowned scholars in their field and even well-established academics still brag on their curriculum vitae about who supervised their PhD endeavour many years ago.

This focus on star professors as supervisors is understandable. First, a star professor as a supervisor indeed signals quality. After all, a star professor is unlikely to work with a PhD student they think may lack talent. Second, the star professor's networks are likely to open many doors for you. The star professor may be asked to write a commentary for a prestigious newspaper, but lacks the time to scribble it down. They may then ask you to write it and co-publish it with you. Alternatively, the star professor may be invited to present some of their work at a conference. Yet they may lack the time to attend, and send you instead. Even if their direct networks will not open doors for you, the star professor's brand will. If you choose to enter the academic labour market upon graduation, few items will boost the value of your application as much as an authoritative recommendation from a star professor.

Try this ... for finding an early career supervisor

- Create a long list of potential PhD supervisors
- Focus on those who are early career scholars
- Due diligence those who have published at least five articles in the past three years with their PhD student(s)

However, the famous supervisor can be problematic for the PhD student hoping to pursue a lean PhD. After all, this lean PhD requires much time investment from the supervisor who usually provides the first round of feedback (and then feedback again and again) on the work produced by the student. The star professor may be too busy to provide this kind of supervision. And even if they are not too busy, they just may not be interested in investing much time in the PhD student. After all, the star professor has already established a stellar reputation. No papers co-authored with a PhD student are required to maintain it. Indeed, a friend of mine who wrote his PhD with a star professor at Oxford University complained that he would only see his supervisor every five to six months – and that it would take just as long until the supervisor would provide feedback on a draft by my friend.

The early career supervisor may be more suitable for pursuing a lean PhD. They are likely to be less busy than the star professor. Furthermore, they need to churn out more papers to advance their reputation and a PhD student can contribute to this. Hence, it is in the interest of the supervisor to provide thorough and continuous feedback on an MVP. You need to watch out, though, that the supervisor does not leverage you too much for building their reputation. You deserve the credit for the work you have done, not your supervisor. This means, for instance, that you must always be the lead author if you have done most work for a paper that you developed with your supervisor, even if they are pushing you to go second. Both of my PhD supervisors were (relatively) early career scholars when I started my PhD with them. I met with both separately on a weekly basis at the beginning of my PhD to shape my endeavour, usually receiving feedback on early drafts within a few days.

It can be difficult to tell when launching a PhD if a supervisor will invest the needed time in you or not.[93] A star professor may turn out to be extremely invested in a PhD student, providing feedback again and again to help them to shape the work. Meanwhile, the early career supervisor may only pursue single-authored works and show little interest in their PhD students. It may thus be an advisable risk diversification strategy to have more than one supervisor for your PhD if your university allows this. Indeed, you may even have a star professor as well as an early career supervisor working with you on your research to leverage the different advantages that these two types of supervisor offer. A reliable indication of the potential of a supervisor from a lean PhD perspective can be their publication list. If this features many recent pieces written with PhD students, the supervisor is likely to be a promising choice. The prospective PhD student may also reach out to PhD students of the potential supervisor who are often listed on the supervisor's website. Conducting such due diligence on a supervisor is not uncommon. In fact, prospective PhD students of one of my supervisors frequently reach out to me to learn how it was to work with her during my PhD (and potential PhD students I consider working with also talk to my current PhD students to figure out if I am a match for them).

If you ended up with a supervisor that turns out to be a 'lemon' despite your various due diligence measures, countermeasures need to be undertaken. After all, the supervisor is a central player for implementing the lean PhD approach. However, caution is needed when choosing countermeasures. Any specific academic market you operate in is miniscule and peers will know if issues with your supervisor have arisen. Since your supervisor has been in the market much longer than you, the dominant narrative regarding these issues may eventually be that you are the one who is difficult to work with, not your supervisor.

First, it can be advisable to add an additional supervisor to your PhD if you struggle with your current supervisor (or add a third one if you already have two supervisors and you are struggling with both). This is the most face-saving move for all parties involved and thus the one that I would most recommend. The reason that can be communicated for adding a supervisor can be content-driven; the additional supervisor has an expertise needed for your PhD that your current supervisor does not have (to that extent). One of my friends who did not get along with her PhD supervisor took this countermeasure. She then started working a lot more with the additional supervisor which allowed her to progress again in her PhD endeavour.

If it is impossible to add a supervisor and shift your focus to them and the situation with your existing supervisor(s) remains unbearable, terminating the relationship may be the option of last resort. Terminating the relationship with your supervisor(s) can even imply that you quit your PhD. I discuss this option

> ### Insights from a PhD researcher
>
> I have been doing research in a research associate role for almost three years now and I am about to embark on a PhD. I will most definitely go for an early career supervisor for this, given my past experiences. Indeed, I have been reporting to an early career supervisor at the Institute of Water Policy, National University of Singapore, ever since I joined academia and it has been a wonderful experience so far. Together, my supervisor and I have published several newspaper articles, we have jointly written four policy briefs and even drafted two journal articles. My supervisor has so much drive and energy and she has helped me so much with providing extremely detailed feedback to shape these outputs. I do not think that any star professor would have invested this much time. I already have a wide range of publications prior to applying to my PhD which I think will be a significant advantage in the application process. If you are also considering doing a PhD, I really recommend going for the early career supervisor instead of the star professor. It will only benefit you along the way.
>
> **Udisha Saklani, (incoming) PhD Student (Public Policy), National University of Singapore, Singapore**

in Section 4.6. If you are keen to continue your PhD, an alternative supervisor is needed before you take any concrete steps regarding termination with your existing supervisor(s). Once the termination is made public, the narrative can swing against you and it will be very difficult to find another supervisor, particularly if your current supervisor is a star in the field.

▶ 2.5 Embracing the paper route

The main means of generating quality in the lean start-up approach is rapid prototyping. This requires an MVP that contains the core features of the envisaged product. The MVP frequently only focuses on just a single feature,[94] since the time required for an envisaged end user to provide feedback on this single feature is usually much less than the time required to provide feedback on the entire product. The equivalent of collecting feedback from an end user on an entire product in the world of the academy is the collecting of feedback on an entire thesis. While communication in the public sphere is becoming snappier, the traditional PhD format, the full thesis, has remained largely unchanged in the past few decades in most countries of the world.[95]

An alternative to the traditional thesis is the paper route (the paper route is also called 'PhD by published works' or 'PhD by publication' in some countries).

This route is said to have become more popular in recent years, although no statistics are available to back this claim.[96] The paper route usually requires the PhD researcher to write between three and five papers.[97] Many universities – such as Oxford University and most universities in the Netherlands – require the PhD student who opts for this route to write four papers. Meanwhile, most universities in Germany only require three papers. Research papers in the social sciences are typically between 6,000 words and 8,000 words, including references, in most social sciences. Literature review papers can exceed 10,000 words. Meanwhile, papers in the natural sciences are shorter on average. For instance, articles that report novel findings in *Advanced Materials*, a prestigious natural science journal, are around 3,000 words.[98]

Many universities, particularly in continental Europe, do not allow the paper route yet.[99] Meanwhile, several disciplines – particularly within the humanities – are sceptical of it. If you start screening potential universities and disciplines for your PhD, dropping those that do not allow the paper route can boost your PhD endeavour. Many professors also continue to view the PhD via a traditional thesis to be the only legitimate route towards the achievement of this degree even if their universities allow the paper route in principle.[96,99] I would check during the very first conversation with a potential supervisor if the paper route can be implemented with them. If the potential supervisor is critical towards the paper route, this can be one reason for not choosing this specific supervisor but rather one that embraces the paper route.

The lean PhD approach is at least somewhat at odds with the traditional thesis. The main reason for the paper route from the perspective of the lean PhD is that papers – as relatively compact units of your work – are extremely helpful for rapid prototyping. Rapid prototyping requires time from your end users, but this time is scarce in contemporary academia. Hence, you may struggle to collect thorough feedback on your integrated thesis, which can be 80,000 words or longer, in a reasonable amount of time.[95,100] Meanwhile, collecting this kind of feedback on a 6,000-word paper is likely to be a much more accomplishable quest.

Since a paper is shorter than a full thesis, the chances that it is read – the precondition for both academic and societal impact – are also much greater. Admittedly, papers do not often receive much attention either. The average scholarly article is read in its entirety by 10 people.[101] As a consequence, 82 per cent of articles published in the humanities, 32 per cent of articles in the social sciences and 27 per cent of articles in the natural sciences are not even cited once.[102] Current citations of my papers suggest that even those citing you may not have read your work. There is no other way to explain some of the citations I have received. (Data on the average number of citations for a PhD thesis is not available.)

Another reason for the paper route is that PhD students choosing this route will also spend much less time writing which can be a draining activity for many. After all, a paper PhD is considerably more compact than the traditional thesis. In addition to the papers, students are usually required to write a supporting statement which mostly comprises an introduction, reflection on methods, a literature review and a conclusion. This supporting statement is 12,000 words on average, including references.[96] Some universities require only about 5,000 words.[96] A paper PhD with four papers, each of 7,000 words, and a 12,000-word supporting statement would thus only be 40,000 words, whereas a short full thesis would be around 60,000 words. If you manage to write around 500 words of publishable material per day, you save 40 working days of writing via the paper PhD. Admittedly, you may spend more time on data collection in the paper PhD since it is frequently not written on a single dataset but on multiple datasets. I discuss in Chapter 3 how you can be as efficient as possible about this data collection.

Multiple datasets for one PhD can also be a risk mitigation strategy. The traditional full thesis is usually built around a single idea. The risk of research failure is thus also concentrated on this single idea and this risk can be considerable, given the uncertainty associated with conducting original research, as discussed in Chapter 1. It is also possible that the assessors of your thesis may not like the specific idea you explored in it even if it was executed soundly. Meanwhile, the paper route allows the PhD student to investigate several separate research ideas within a theme. Even if one or two ideas fail to reveal meaningful results, there are still plenty of research ideas left within the research project whose execution may work out. Furthermore, the assessors have more ideas within a thesis to sympathize with when judging it.

Most universities do not require that your papers are accepted or published in peer-reviewed journals for you to complete your PhD. Rather, the papers need to be 'publication-worthy', according to the assessors of your thesis.[103] This is a helpful ruling since the peer-review process can be uncontrollably lengthy at times. For instance, I once waited more than six months for reviews from a journal on one of my papers. If you manage to publish one or two of the papers in your PhD thesis in a scholarly journal despite the lengthy review process prior to submission, this will be a major boost for you. First, it is extremely difficult to impossible for assessors to turn down a thesis that includes material already published in recognized journals since a peer-reviewed article is widely seen as the gold medal of academic achievement.[104] Furthermore, peer-reviewed articles listed on your curriculum vitae will greatly impress those within and outside of academia when you apply for jobs. These are additional reasons for the paper route.

Lastly, papers make it much easier to work in teams. I explain in Section 3.3 why this can accelerate your PhD, while boosting its impact and quality.

▶ **2.6 Creative resourcing**

Assume you have found a promising niche research topic you are excited about and an early career supervisor at a prestigious university who is equally excited about it. You have developed and submitted a research proposal based on the lean approach, you have been admitted to your dream university and you are pumped about starting your paper-based PhD. The one remaining question for the launch phase of your PhD is: how can you finance the next few years of your life?

The lean start-up approach has been frequently outlined as helping the business venture to cut costs.[105] And the MVP approach is indeed much more cost-efficient than the original approach to building business ventures, as outlined in Chapter 1. However, lean start-ups are also famous for their creative approach to gathering resources. Lean start-ups have discovered crowdfunding as a major source of income in recent years. Crowdfunding is gathering tiny amounts of funding from a large number of (mostly private) individuals, usually via platforms such as Kickstarter,[106] the world's largest crowdfunding platform, or GoFundMe.[107] The traditional alternative is relying on a few institutional investors that are frequently 'growth-obsessed'[108] and thus dictate terms that only aim for the rapid initial public offering (IPO) of the business venture. Over USD 3 billion were raised via crowdfunding in 2016 in the United States alone.[109] Meanwhile, the World Bank has predicted that crowdfunding investments will total USD 85 billion a year in developing countries in 2025.[110]

Try this … for finding funding for your PhD

- Discuss with your friends if a crowdsourcing campaign may work for your PhD
- Create a list of all PhD scholarships (including application deadlines) you are eligible for
- Call your supervisor for advice

Goldman Sachs, an investment bank, has called crowdfunding 'the most disruptive of all of the new models in finance'.[111] Anecdotal evidence suggests that it may even offer opportunities for PhD students. A three-year doctorate at the University of Oxford costs GBP 22,500 just to cover university tuition and college fees. Eleri Anona Watson, a current PhD student at the University of Oxford, just did not have this money despite working in several jobs. She thus decided to launch a crowdfunding campaign to help her cover costs. She pitched her PhD by offering 'access to an exclusive blog where I keep you up-to-date with my progress, discuss my writing, interesting quotes, lectures and books I'm reading' for those contributing GBP 10 to her PhD. She offered a 'personal letter for every month of my DPhil and a Skype conversation about my work' for those contributing GBP 500.[112] Overall, Eleri managed to raise GBP 3,671 from 38 people via this campaign – almost 20 per cent of the university tuition and college fees, a considerable achievement.

The ambition of Eleri's PhD is to create a new framework for queer and feminist theory. Beyond her PhD, Eleri is also working as an activist to promote women's career advancement in academia. Most of those funding Eleri did not share their reasons for doing so. Those who did offer reasons seem to identify particularly with her engagement for women and academia and wanted to support this via their funding. For instance, supporter Hannah Gwenllian wrote that 'I really enjoy reading your posts on Facebook about all the positive work you are doing surrounding women in academia. Keep at it!'. Hannah thus belongs to the third archetype of crowdfunding investors, the 'affinity funder'.

Crowdfunding investors can be distinguished into friends and family investors who are motivated by the desire to support a friend or family member; consumer investors who are keen for the end product promised by the business endeavour; affinity funders who are motivated by a shared interest, passion, belief or identity; and financial investors who are motivated by a potential financial return.[113] If you find the idea of (at least partially) crowdfunding your PhD appealing, you may want to think through which of these archetypes you may appeal to most and how to then best frame your pitch towards this group. For instance, you may work on a PhD that undertakes a comparative study of drivers and characteristics of urban gardening in Europe. Urban gardening is a niche topic that has many fervent fans and thus there is a potential for acquiring consumer investors. You could promise potential funders to send a draft chapter of your thesis every three to four months to appeal to their interest in your end product.

I did not run a crowdfunding campaign for my PhD. Luckily, I received financial support from a consulting firm, my former employer, throughout my studies as well as the German government – two institutional investors from the lean start-up perspective. Both sources of finance are worth exploring for any prospective PhD students. First, companies may be interested in funding an employee's PhD if this is relevant for their business models. Consultancies in Germany frequently offer employees educational leave to pursue a PhD due to the standing of a doctorate in the country. The PhD signals intellectuality and respectability in Germany – preconditions for advising senior management. A risk in securing funding from a corporation is their likely 'application obsession', the academic equivalent of the growth obsession of institutional investors that fund start-ups. While this will likely boost the practical quality and impact of your PhD, your academic quality and impact may suffer. I outline how to address this trade-off between academic and practical quality and impact in Section 4.5 of this book.

Second, many governments around the world offer schemes for their students to pursue a PhD. Several governments even run specific schemes to enable students to study at particularly prestigious universities abroad (which is another reason to go for prestigious universities).[114] Even when such specific programmes are not offered, the student applying for a PhD scholarship in a general programme will have a decent chance of it being awarded if they have already secured a PhD spot at a prestigious university. Government scholarships are usually not tied to applicability. Their main downside is the limited funding provided by most of them.

I compared the PhD supervisor earlier in this chapter to the business angel of a start-up. Indeed, your supervisor may also be a powerful ally in search for funding, particularly if they are not at a prestigious university and/or working on a hyped research topic. While writing this, I research and teach at Utrecht University. The institution is reputable in my research theme, sustainable development, and I also now focus on a hyped topic, the circular economy, as outlined earlier. However, Utrecht University is not comparable to Oxford University, the University of Cambridge or the MIT and this creates difficulties in recruiting gifted students, despite my focus on a hyped topic. Any suitable student I find I thus support as much as I can by securing funding.

The most common source for PhD funding in some countries, including Germany, is working as a research associate for one's supervisor throughout the PhD. However, this model can be problematic, with PhD students usually hired on part-time contracts. However, the work allocated to them can frequently not be completed in part-time hours. Too little time is then left for the PhD and the endeavour drags on and on and on. The model can be advisable for some candidates if the student is offered a 25 per cent contract and if the tasks allocated to them then only take 25 per cent of their time per week to complete, since this job can help the student to structure their day. However, if you can finance your PhD without taking up a research associateship, this is always the preferred option from my point of view.

3 Executing the PhD

This chapter explains:

- Why you need to aim to develop minimum viable papers throughout the execution phase of your PhD
- Why writing is more important than reading while executing the PhD
- How building teams can be helpful to your PhD
- What types of low-cost experimentation can support your PhD endeavour most
- How academic conferences can help you progress in your PhD
- Why it is sometimes necessary to change the topic of your PhD while writing it

▶ 3.1 The minimum viable paper (and: the value of rejections)

Lean methodologies are popular among many start-ups around the world, as outlined in Chapter 1. Yet with the success of the lean movement, critics emerged as well. One of the possibly most viable criticisms concerns the difficulty of collecting thorough feedback. One entrepreneur who raised this criticism is John Finneran. John tried to launch a software firm via the lean start-up approach. This firm aimed to simplify how non-profits plan and measure their social and environmental impacts. Yet the company failed; the main reason was, according to John, that the firm was unable to collect the needed feedback to improve its minimum viable product (MVP). 'The [MVP] preached by [the lean start-up movement] has limited practical use. Our clients were [...] too irritated [by our MVP] to "iterate" [it] with us.' 'Customers aren't interested in funding your "learning". They want reliable software [from Day 1] that delivers value consistently,'[115] John recounts on his blog.

One of my friends from Oxford, Huw, found that this experience from start-up entrepreneurs also holds true in academia. He wrote a paper on a water megaproject in Asia as part of his research. For this paper, he managed to obtain feedback from seven scholars prior to submitting this work to a journal – this is an extraordinary amount of feedback. I recently asked three colleagues to provide feedback for one of my manuscripts – only one did (she is also my girl-friend). Academics are not always generous with their time. Upon submission of his work to a journal, Huw also received anonymous feedback from three more scholars. 'The feedback the anonymous scholars provided was so much more thorough than any feedback I had received earlier on,' he shared with me after the publication of the paper. 'It was the feedback from these anonymous scholars that really helped to improve my paper.'

PhDs and promotions are awarded for the publication of peer-reviewed work, the gold medal in the race of academic achievement. Yet your scholarly colleagues will not let you win this medal without providing you with major challenges along the way. Once your paper is out for review, you are close to the finishing line of the race. Your scholarly colleagues, most of whom are fair players, according to my experience, will toughen up then and undertake a final major effort to prevent you from winning (called 'major revision' in the peer-review process). This is the incisive feedback that will improve the robustness of your work if incorporated. If you approach peer reviewers prior to submission, feedback provision is like a training exercise – nobody goes all in – but it will pro-vide you with some friendly guidance which can help you to prepare for the race. Hence, it makes sense to collect it – you need training to succeed. But the race has not even started if your paper is not submitted to a peer-reviewed journal. And you are all about the race.

Feedback from anonymous journal reviewers can be tough. An article in BuzzFeed featured some of the most brutal comments from reviewers. One reviewer allegedly wrote that 'it is early in the year, but difficult to imagine any paper overtaking this one for lack of imagination, logic, or data – it is beyond redemption'. Another review was said to report: 'This paper adds nothing to the existing knowledge of the subject.'[116] Articles like this only result in many PhD students being intimidated by journal submissions. Consequently, these students will try to hone their paper over many months and sometimes even years. This is one important reason why many PhDs take so long, in my view – students wait too long to collect the valuable anonymous feedback from scholars that can guide their work. Lean methodologies suggest that a paper must be submitted to a journal sooner rather than later. After all, the peer reviewer of a journal is the end user of the execution phase of the PhD and thus at the core of iteration. The earlier you submit your paper to a journal, the sooner you will receive the most valuable feedback to further improve it.

It is difficult to gauge when a paper is ready to be submitted. On the one hand, you want the paper to be good enough not to be rejected by the reviewers – a rejection after reviews which takes at least three months in the social sciences to reach you (I recently waited six months for a rejection from one journal) and up to two months in the natural sciences significantly delays the eventual publication, since you will have to wait just as long for reviews from another journal. Reviews after the first or second revision are provided much more quickly since much time is lost in the first round of peer review in finding scholars willing to review your work; once willing reviewers are identified, these usually provide feedback rather quickly. On the other hand, you do not want the paper to be perfect; you want it to be a minimum viable paper, since reviewers will always provide plentiful comments on any paper, no matter how excellent it already is. After all, this is their very task as reviewers.

A PhD student at Oxford University once shared with me a rule of thumb which I find helpful, on how to gauge the suitability of a paper for submission. His supervisor refused to iterate a manuscript more than three times with any student. 'If I provide thorough feedback on your paper three times and you then truly attempt to incorporate this feedback three times, this is as good as this paper gets with the two of us working on it', the supervisor allegedly said. Indeed, I know of supervisors who iterate papers with students dozens of times. Iterating a single paper over many months or even years can be extremely frustrating for students who are keen to progress in their PhDs. And there are many instances of these papers still being rejected by journals. Thus, thoroughly iterating a paper no more than three times prior to submission to a journal sounds like a sensible course of action to me and I cannot recall any paper throughout my PhD that I iterated more than three times. Indeed, there are diminishing marginal benefits for every additional round of revisions on a paper, I find.

Iterating a specific paper no more than three times is one of the criteria I use to determine its submission readiness. I am listing the other criteria in Table 3.1 (the more 'Yes'es you collect, the greater the submission readiness of your work). For instance, I see too many footnotes as an indication that you may have worked on your paper for too long. After all, these footnotes are usually only mere asides to your work. Your paper will never be rejected just because you did not include every single possible side point in your account. I also strongly believe in gut feeling, but this really depends on your level of self-confidence.[117] If you feel that you are reasonably self-critical (not overly critical!) *and* you have a generally positive gut feeling about your paper, this can be a helpful indication that you may submit now. I will revisit some of the questions in Table 3.1, for example those on conferences, in the subsequent sections of this chapter.

Table 3.1 'Is your paper ready for submission?' checklist

#	Question	Answer
1	Have you done at least three rounds of revisions with your supervisor(s) on your paper?	
2	Do you still have less than five footnotes in your paper?	
3	Have you received positive feedback on your paper at a conference?	
4	Do you have a generally positive gut feeling about this paper?	
5	Have you worked on the paper for more than six months?	
6	Can you no longer view this paper with a degree of objectivity?	
7	Has this paper been through copy-editing?	

Even very thorough papers can and will be rejected due to the randomness inherent in the peer-review process. Numerous studies have examined what scholars call 'inter-coder reliability' – the amount of agreement between different reviewers giving ratings to the same paper. If peer review was entirely objective, these ratings should not differ at all and inter-coder reliability should thus be high. However, this is not the case. A study summarizing the results of 84 previous studies that examined inter-coder reliability, published between 1966 and 2008, found that it is usually low. The authors of the study write that 'the reviewers agreed in their evaluations for [only] 17% more of the manuscripts than would have been predicted on the basis of chance alone'.[118] Peer review can almost be as random as a coin toss.[119]

Several of my papers have been rejected, and when this happens any scholar likes to blame this on the randomness of the peer-review process. However, I feel, upon reconsideration, that most of my papers were rejected because they were not good enough yet. The reviewer that recommended rejecting one of my papers wrote that 'a critical part of the argument [...] is buried. [The authors are] sometimes getting lost in another argument that doesn't seem to be really where they want to go'. Upon reading the paper again, I realized that the reviewer was correct. This was thus a valuable rejection. I spent a month rewriting the paper based on the detailed feedback of the reviewer. This was my build-measure-learn loop. I then resubmitted it to another journal, more prestigious than the one I originally had sent the manuscript to, and the piece was published less than five months afterwards – an unusually fast schedule for scholarly publications in the social sciences. This paper is now one of the publications I am most proud of, and I write in its acknowledgements: 'Lastly, we are also grateful for the constructive comments of three anonymous reviewers from *Global Environmental Change* as well as the comments of three anonymous reviewers from *Social Movement Studies* who rejected a previous version of this paper.'[120]

Not all disciplines and universities allow a paper-based PhD, as discussed earlier. However, the feedback provided by anonymous reviewers is of such tremendous help that I suggest even to those who cannot write a paper-based PhD to submit chapters from their thesis as papers to journals to boost their PhD's quality. Admittedly, rewriting a chapter from a full thesis into a paper is time-consuming. However, the quality boost and thus also the impact boost your work will experience via anonymous peer review is worth it. Furthermore, any peer-reviewed publication from your doctoral work signals the quality of your doctorate which, in turn, ensures that you will pass, while also increasing your chances of finding an academic job. I further discuss this in Chapter 4 of this book.

When iterating the manuscript of this book with PhD students prior to its publication, I was asked if the concept of the minimum viable paper would be equivalent to that of the least publishable unit (LPU). The LPU concept refers to a publication strategy that produces papers which contain the smallest amount of information that can generate a publication in a peer-reviewed journal.[121] Some also call this strategy 'scientific salami slicing'.[122] The concept of the minimum viable paper is different to the LPU. It differs both in its aims and in its perspective on the reviewer. The LPU approach spreads insights over multiple papers since it aims to produce as many papers as possible; quality and impact are not central to this approach. Reviewers are only seen as barriers, delaying publication. Meanwhile, the aim of the lean PhD approach, and thus the minimum viable paper as one component of this approach, is to produce quality research and impact which is enabled by comprehensive and incisive pieces of work. Iteration with anonymous reviewers is one main tool for producing these types of accounts during the execution phase of the PhD and their feedback is thus taken very seriously.

I now complete the first draft of my research papers (once all data is collected) very quickly, usually within one week; I had also tried to work at this speed during my doctorate. I submit my papers after a maximum of three rounds of iteration with my co-authors and I admit that the incorporation of my co-authors' feedback is often 'quick and dirty'. Indeed, I had a co-author complain to me recently that I 'took the path of very least resistance' when incorporating her feedback. However, I turn into a perfectionist once the anonymous reviews are in. I know that my colleagues have provided the most incisive feedback on my work via these anonymous reviews which, if incorporated by me, will boost my work's quality and impact. Indeed, I take the feedback of reviewers so seriously that I often take longer to incorporate their feedback than I take for the initial write-up of the full paper. For instance, I produced a 26-page response letter (alongside a comprehensively revised manuscript) to the reviewers who provided comments on an article that was later published in *Global Environmental Change*, one of the most prestigious journals on environmental issues.[88]

Try this ... for embracing the minimum viable paper approach

- Try to complete the first draft of your paper very quickly
- Submit your paper to a journal after three rounds of revisions
- Become a perfectionist once the feedback from the journal is in

---

I usually start incorporating feedback by putting all of it in a single Excel sheet. I then start with the comments that seem most straightforward to implement – this gives me the feeling of really progressing. I close with the trickiest comments, which I find are mostly comments that demand changes to the structure of the entire paper. Most importantly, I really develop in-depth responses to every single comment raised by my reviewers in my revision process. I re-read the entire paper several times once all comments are incorporated to make sure that it still flows and I always wait one day before I give the paper what I call the 'final read'. This one-day break helps me to develop a fresh look at the paper. After the final read, I send the paper off to copy-editing to make sure no more typos and formatting issues are left. My girlfriend was my copy-editing agency during my PhD, but you might want to use a professional copy-editing agency if you can, since not all girlfriends and boyfriends are likely to be great copy-editors.

▶ 3.2 Writing as learning

The lean start-up approach is about learning-by-doing. A LinkedIn post by Josh Fechter, a serial entrepreneur, may ideally summarize this. Fechter writes:

> I read 120 books in a year. I documented the entire process online. And I learned something valuable. Execution matters more. In a month and a half [of execution], I learnt more than from reading the 120 books. [...] You won't find the answers [...] in a book.

The typical PhD student will intuitively adopt the techniques during their PhD that helped them to succeed during their undergraduate and graduate studies, with the likely main technique being lots and lots of reading. This student will spend months and months in the beginning of the PhD reading scholarly literature. However, little is usually gained by this. Most importantly, many students are likely to soon forget the majority of what they read (this certainly holds true for me), with reading thus becoming a never-ending task.

Rapid prototyping suggests that progress towards the final product occurs by iterating prototypes again and again. Ideally, the final product of the PhD student in the execution phase of the PhD is an accepted paper published in a peer-reviewed journal. It can also be a full thesis for those that have been unable to choose the paper route. Both formats imply, though, that PhD students must start writing as soon as possible. Hence, the mindset to be adopted for the lean PhD is: read only as much as necessary, write as soon as possible. Advancing the scholarly literature, the core task for the PhD student, requires understanding what this literature has examined and then identifying a research gap based on this understanding. However, it is usually sufficient to closely read a book's or an article's abstract (and sometimes also the conclusion), while skimming the remainder of the article, to gauge what the piece is (not) about. Only very few articles are extremely close to the paper or thesis the PhD student will eventually write. These are the only ones that the PhD student needs to read most carefully.

There is an unmanageable amount of information out there on almost any topic imaginable. Up to 1.5 million peer-reviewed articles are published annually.[101] Hence, it is important for the PhD student to be strategic about what to read – and even about what to just skim. I usually zoom in on those articles first that are widely cited – after all, the number of citations are the most dominant indicator for academic impact, as discussed previously. The academic search engine Scopus allows you to sort your search results based on citations and it is thus the search engine I usually choose to start any literature review. Others start their literature reviews via reading through articles on their topic that are published in the most prestigious journals in their fields. I advise against this, since most articles published in even the most prestigious peer-reviewed journals exert extremely little influence in their fields. Indeed, only 15 per cent of articles published in any journal (including *Nature* or *Science*) account for more than 50 per cent of that journal's total citations.[123,124]

Much scholarly literature from psychology also emphasizes that writing is superior to reading when attempting to build knowledge and understanding of a specific topic.[125-128] One observation within this literature is that 'better writers tend to be better readers',[128] according to psychologist Sandra Stotsky, since the writing reader 'can begin to make informed guesses about how to use the ideas or discourse features of a given text in light of his or her goals as a writer', as psychologist Stuart Greene explains.[126] In other words: you have a clearer idea of what you are looking for in a text you are reading when you are already writing.

Once I had developed an initial idea regarding a paper during my doctorate, I usually started by developing a storyboard. A storyboard is only a loose collection of bullet points that build upon each other, summarizing the key story I aim to tell in the paper. There are already sub-sections in my storyboard as well as hard data in sub-bullets, mostly facts from studies that relate to my topic to back my ideas in the main bullet points. I also include quotes from other articles or interviews as sub-bullet points. This helps me to quickly flesh out ideas later. Every main bullet point represents one main idea and thus one paragraph. A well-developed storyboard contains around 40 main bullet points which then, if developed further, equates to an article of 6,000 words with the average length of an academic paragraph being 150 words.[129]

I recently told one of my colleagues at Utrecht University about my storyboard approach. She said: 'I don't think I could ever be so systematic about developing a paper. This sounds really difficult.' I admit that it can be tricky to work with this approach in the beginning. Starters may find it easiest to first develop bullet points for their results section in the storyboard. After all, the results dictate the story. From there, you may move on to the discussion section and then to the introduction to develop the hook of your paper. You can then continue with the section 'Highlights', since it forces you to really carve out the core messages of your work. If you have written down the 'Highlights', you have really cut the Gordian knot. The theory section may still offer some challenges, but the methods and conclusion are then almost effortless.

Once my storyboard is complete, I start developing this into a research outline. This outline contains full paragraphs, with its total length usually being around 3,000 words. My research outline includes the same structure as my storyboard. I frame my work in the introduction and this framing usually does not change much until the submission of my paper to a journal. Meanwhile, I exactly detail in the section 'Methods' how I intend to go about my research. This helps to ensure that my chosen approach is as thought-through as possible. For instance, I outline in this section how many interviews I intend to conduct and why, whom to interview, my plan A on how to contact these interviewees, my plan B on how to contact them, etc. I review and critically discuss relevant theoretical literature in the theory section.

Try this ... for writing as learning

- Create a storyboard for your first paper once you have started reading on your topic
- Turn your storyboard into a research outline as soon as possible
- Create the first full draft of your paper while in the middle of your data collection

My initial hypotheses regarding results are outlined in the section 'Results'. This developing of hypotheses prior to conducting research is also driven by the lean start-up approach. The lean canvas, mentioned in the beginning of Chapter 2 of this book, asks the start-up entrepreneur to formulate hypotheses regarding its various buckets. These are then tested via rapid prototyping. Formulating hypotheses forces you to nuance your thinking about the potential narrative you want to eventually put forward in your paper from Day 1. Any great paper in the social sciences depends on this narrative and there is also a need for a narrative in the natural sciences. Thus, you want to think about your narrative as thoroughly as possible early on. Formulating hypotheses also helps to ensure that your data collection is as targeted as possible and so cuts waste.

Around 25 per cent of people think mostly in words. Developing written hypotheses to reflect upon their upcoming research is thus most suitable for PhD students belonging to this group. Meanwhile, 30 per cent of the population thinks mostly in images and 45 per cent via a mix of words and images.[130] Those who are more inclined towards images may benefit from developing hypotheses via visualizations. I think both in words and images and thus I have usually tried to combine written hypotheses with visualizations when developing hypotheses. I would often start out with a visualization depicting the main sub-themes to be explored and I would then develop written hypotheses around these various sub-themes. Figure 3.1 shows a visualization that I developed during the first week of my doctorate on the various socio-economic impacts of large dams.

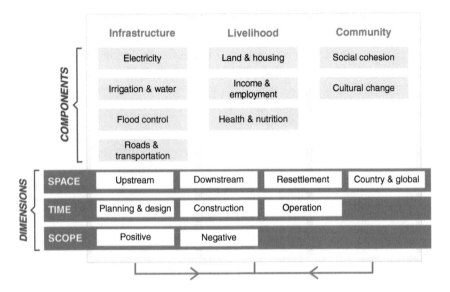

Figure 3.1 Example of a visualization[78]

I would usually iterate my research outline with both of my supervisors to sharpen it prior to the data collection. I would continue writing even during the data collection phase, developing what I call a version-1.0 paper. For instance, I continued writing once I had carried out around 20 interviews for one of my papers. I attempted to write the entire paper based on these interviews (around 40 interviews are considered a comprehensive dataset for this type of paper in my field). This helped me to gauge what information I was lacking to advance my manuscript. I also shared this draft with one of my supervisors. This second opinion pointed me towards more gaps in the data I had collected. Thanks to this write-up and the feedback I was more targeted in the subsequent interviews and could thus progress efficiently.

None of the various drafts I wrote during data collection were more than drafts, my minimum viable papers, and I was also explicit about this with my supervisors. Focusing on creating drafts instead of polished products can vastly accelerate the writing process. After all, many PhD students struggle with overcoming a writer's block. The core reason for this writer's block is the belief that anything written by a PhD student must be of the quality of a PhD.[131] This is simply not the case. Only the final thesis needs to be of PhD quality and one will reach this quality by producing drafts and iterating these again and again. Conceptualizing anything that you write as a draft can minimize the pressures you experience as a PhD student.

Insights from a PhD researcher

Writing drafts as soon as possible with the intention of gathering feedback that then boosts the quality of your work is useful advice, but it can be challenging to implement. I feel extremely uncomfortable when sharing work with others that I do not consider to be finished since I am quite a perfectionist. Therefore, I had to gather all my courage to share a paper with my supervisor that was only a draft from my point of view. This helped me a lot, though. First, my supervisor thought that the paper I had provided was far developed already. This was not only encouraging, but it also helped me to adjust my perceptions of quality. At the same time, my supervisor provided some structural feedback on one of the sections in the paper that I had not anticipated. I could have honed the paper for another month or two without going in the direction he suggested. I was happy that I did not. After all, there are few things for a PhD student that are as frustrating as rewriting a paper (or some sections of it) that you consider to be complete already. A paper – even when published in a peer-reviewed journal – is always work in progress. Having understood this early on in my PhD has really accelerated my PhD journey.

Sarah Tiba, PhD Student (Innovation Studies), Utrecht University, the Netherlands

A second strategy to overcome writer's block can be to write the story-board, the research outline and/or your various drafts by hand instead of writing on a computer. While typing something into your computer may feel much faster and less tedious, and thus more productive, many find that writing by hand is more natural and thus facilitates the start of the writing process in particular.[132] After all, we all started as writers with pen and paper. I also frequently write by hand. Indeed, many paragraphs in this book were first scribbled down on a piece of paper before being further sharpened on a computer screen.

▶ 3.3 Academia as team sport (or: the end of the 'lone scholar')

The myth of the single start-up founder has been propagated for decades.[133,134] However, co-founding is common these days. A 2016 analysis of data from CrunchBase, a start-up directory, revealed that the average number of founders is 1.85 per start-up.[135] Indeed, more and more thought leaders on start-ups now attack the myth of the single founder. Paul Graham, one of the most influential voices on start-ups, wrote an article titled 'The 18 Mistakes That Kill Startups'.[134] The first mistake that he outlines is being a single founder. He goes on to explain that the single founder lacks the partner with whom to iterate and thus improve ideas – essential to successfully launch a start-up, according to the lean start-up approach. Indeed, research showcases that start-ups with two founders are 19 per cent less likely to scale prematurely,[135] while achieving almost three times the user growth on average of the single founder start-up.[136] Investors are also more trusting towards start-ups that are co-founded. These start-ups raise 30 per cent more on average than single founder start-ups.[136]

Most PhD students tend to think of the PhD as a lone undertaking (with sporadic inputs from the supervisor) since the academy frequently evokes the idea of the 'lone scholar' just as frequently as the start-up community evokes the idea of the single start-up founder. However, the 'lone scholar' is under attack in academia just as much as the 'single start-up founder' is in the world of entrepreneurship.[26] Indeed, academia has become a team sport in recent years. The first issue of the German academic journal *Der Naturforscher*, published in 1774, only featured single-authored works.[137] By 1900, about 7 per cent of papers in biology, chemistry and physics had co-authors, and the time of teamwork had begun.[137,138] Today, almost all articles in the natural sciences are co-authored. By 2000, the average number of authors per paper in medical journals was seven.[137,139] Eighty per cent of works in the social sciences are now also co-authored.[140] The only discipline that still maintains a notable single-author tradition are the humanities. Seventy per cent of articles and book chapters published in the humanities remain single authored.[140]

Co-authoring has become excessive in some disciplines. A recent research paper on the genetic make-up of fruit flies counted 1,014 authors. Some 900 of these authors were undergraduate students who had helped to edit draft genome sequences.[141,142] Physicists currently hold the record for the largest number of contributors to a single research article. A paper in *Physical Review Letters* in 2015 counted 5,154 authors. The research was described on the first nine pages of the article – including references. The remaining 24 pages of the piece listed the authors.[143]

The main reason for co-founding a start-up is to be permanently challenged by a sparring partner. Similarly, the main reason for co-authoring in academia is that these co-authors will challenge your work. If the student offers a scholar co-authorship in exchange for feedback, the feedback provided is likely thorough. After all, the co-author's name will eventually be on the published paper – and thus their academic reputation (and everything is about reputation in the academy) is tied to the collaboration with you. I outlined in Section 2.4 that even the prospective PhD supervisor may be unwilling to provide many rounds of feedback on a research proposal. After all, providing thoughtful feedback requires a lot of time. An important task of the PhD student while executing the lean PhD is to collect thorough feedback on their written work to efficiently boost its quality. Adding co-authors can be an avenue to collecting helpful feedback.

I think of any paper I write as a team project. The initial team of your PhD is your supervisor and you. While you report to your supervisor, I still urge you to think of yourself as the manager of this team. After all, it is your PhD. If you intend to expand this team, those sought for co-authorship ideally complement the skillset of your initial team. For instance, the co-author may master a specific research method that your initial team is not particularly familiar with. Alternatively, the co-author may be an expert in a theory (or may have even developed the theory) that you hope to engage with in your paper and may then write the theory part of your paper. Co-authorship can also be offered in exchange for access to hard-to-reach populations.[144] For instance, I offered co-authorship to a scholar who was able to put me in touch with Chinese dam developers, a stakeholder group almost no scholar has been able to interview.[120] The co-author need not always be an academic. I recently invited consultants from Deloitte to co-author a piece with me. These consultants did not only provide feedback on my drafts to boost my work's applicability for businesses, but also offered access to their client base for my research.

Try this ... for academia as a team sport

- Invite co-authors with specific knowledge, e.g. on a particular method or theory, to your paper project
- Outline the envisaged division of labour upfront
- Recognize that feedback is a gift

If you recruit a co-author for any of the reasons outlined above, it will likely boost the quality and impact of your paper. I already outlined in Chapter 2 how prestige matters in academia and beyond. Prestige can also be a reason to ask a co-author to join a paper since research suggests that reputable journals tend to favour papers which include scholars at elite institutions and/or with PhDs from elite institutions. For instance, one study, published in *Critical Inquiry,* found that 86 per cent of the articles published in the four top journals in the respective field included contributions from scholars at the top 20 per cent of universities. Furthermore, the work found that authors with PhDs from Yale University or Harvard University accounted for 20 per cent of all articles in their sample.[145,146] Inviting reputable co-authors can thus open doors for you that allow publication in the most prestigious journals in your field.

Teams help you to succeed in your PhD. You may also build teams for your research if you write a full thesis rather than a paper PhD. After all, you can always develop a chapter of your full thesis into a paper that can then be authored by several people. Once you turn the paper into a chapter again (a few weeks or months before the submission of your dissertation), you just need to make sure (in most universities) that you acknowledge the work of the various authors that have contributed to your paper. You may also choose to start immediately with a co-authored paper that you then eventually turn into a chapter of your full thesis. While I have not yet heard of any universities that do not allow a multi-authored paper to be turned into a single-authored chapter for a PhD, there may be some. You may thus want to discuss with your institution your plan regarding 'academia as a team sport' for your traditional thesis PhD before you implement it.

If you decide to invite a co-author to your paper project, I recommend that you explicate the envisaged division of labour upfront, otherwise you may both end up frustrated. You may also exercise due diligence on your co-author by talking to those that have previously worked with them. You only want the most excellent co-authors if you envisage a written contribution by them to your work. Sadly, even due diligence does not prevent the freeriding of co-authors. For instance, your co-author may not write the theory part of your paper, although you initially agreed upon this, or they may not contribute the analyses that they were supposed to carry out.

It may also be that your co-author does not provide feedback on your work that makes sense to you. The lean PhD approach is all about cherishing the value of feedback. However, it also recognizes that not all feedback is equally valuable. Indeed, some feedback may not be of any use to you, or it could even be detrimental to the quality of your work. A saying in the field of consulting asserts that 'feedback is a gift'. This saying can also be adopted for the lean PhD approach. It means that while feedback is generally valued, not every piece of feedback (like every gift) needs to be accepted. It can be difficult for a PhD student to gauge the quality of feedback. Ask your supervisors and other more experienced academics for their views if you feel that the feedback provided does not help you to progress.

Do not drop a co-author because of low-quality feedback, however. Indeed, I advise you not to drop a co-author once you have committed to them in any instance (there may be some extreme exceptions to this, of course). Whereas dropping a co-author can be well-deserved, it can also create an antagonist – which could be problematic for you at some point since the academy is a tiny universe. Rather, finish the paper project with the useless co-author as quickly as possible and then make sure that you always have ready a cast-iron excuse to never work with them again.

▶ 3.4 Embracing low-cost experimentation

A start-up founder does not only need a co-founder as well as an advisory board, the start-up community's equivalent to co-authors in academia, to launch their endeavour: most importantly, staff are needed – from the chief marketing officer (CMO) to the controller and the intern. The PhD start-up usually lacks the funding to recruit a full-fledged team of staff. However, some staff can usually be recruited which vastly accelerates the project while boosting its quality and impact. Indeed, there are usually diverse options to create win–win collaborations between your work and that of undergraduate and graduate students – the staff of your PhD start-up.

I worked with multiple students throughout my PhD. I recruited these via my undergraduate university, the University of Münster in Germany, where I teach a course once a year. I worked with a student at first who was keen on co-authoring an academic paper – such a paper polishes any CV. This student, Tim, undertook a variety of tasks throughout the joint development of this paper (which, sadly, did not count towards my PhD). First, he helped to devise the questionnaire we would use to gather data for the paper. Second, he developed a list of possible interviewees. Third, he helped to carry out the interviews. Fourth, he transcribed the various interviews. Fifth, he supported me in searching for suitable literature. Sixth, he even developed – under my guidance – a financial model of a dam project that we eventually presented in the paper. Tim's contribution to this paper[147] cannot be overstated, and working with him saved me much time while contributing to the paper's quality. Evidently, he is a co-author of the paper, and I have mentored him ever since our first collaboration.

The second student I worked with was keen to base her Bachelor's thesis on an original dataset – this, in turn, frequently boosts the grade for the respective thesis. We aligned her thesis topic with the topic of one of my PhD papers so that we could both use the same questionnaire for our work. The student would then support the development of this questionnaire, create a list of possible interviewees, join various interviews and transcribe many of the interviews that were carried out with this questionnaire. Once the peer-reviewed paper with Tim as well as the Bachelor's thesis were completed, I still required research assistance from time to time. I then hired students on an ad hoc basis for this work, which was possible thanks to the funding outlined in Chapter 2.

We tend to maintain the narrative in academia that obtaining a PhD is extremely challenging. While cultivating this narrative, we tend to forget that not all tasks related to a PhD are challenging. Indeed, a variety of typical PhD tasks – from conducting a literature review to transcribing interviews (needed for qualitative PhDs) – could probably be completed by a 16 year old (or someone even younger). These tasks in particular are the ones to delegate. At the same time, we should never underestimate the skills of undergraduate and graduate students. Many are capable enough to already carry out the most complex tasks of a PhD. My best example for this is Tim who as an undergraduate student built a complex financial model of a dam for one of my papers.

Once you have assembled your team of students for a specific paper, a scrum sprint can help organize it. This is probably the most common methodology to organize rapid prototyping, the 'how' of the lean start-up approach.[148] The aim of the scrum sprint is meeting a specific goal that is defined in the beginning of the sprint, e.g. the completion of the first batch of data collection. A timeline, called a 'time box' within the scrum sprint approach, is defined to meet this sprint goal. The most common time box is two weeks, although four weeks may be more advisable for the academic setting at times. Tasks are then defined for this time box for each member of the team, e.g. 'Conduct and transcribe 15 interviews'.

A scrum sprint in a private sector company would entail gathering the entire team every morning for a stand-up meeting. The discomfort of standing for extended periods keeps these meetings brief: typically they do not last longer than 15 minutes. Since the students I worked with were in Germany while I was in the United Kingdom, our stand-up meetings were telephone conversations (and the nature of our tasks did not require us to hold these daily). However, I now try to organize stand-up meetings as frequently as possible in Utrecht. Each team member provides some input, not longer than one minute, which focuses on three questions: first, what did I do yesterday that contributed to meeting the sprint goal? Second, what will I do today to contribute to meeting the sprint goal? And third, do I see any impediment that prevents me or the team from meeting the sprint goal?[149]

Try this ... for embracing low-cost experimentation

- Invite Bachelor's and Master's students to your PhD project
- Organize scrum sprints to manage your teams
- Go digital to cut data collection costs

Admittedly, creating a team that makes sense is more difficult in some disciplines than in others. Delegating data collection tasks to students, in particular, may not be possible for all disciplines. For instance, PhD students in economics tend to rely on extremely large datasets – too large to be created by two or three undergraduate students. However, work can still be delegated to students even in these disciplines. For instance, the PhD student in economics may agree to supervise a graduate student's Master's thesis. If the topic of the Master's thesis is aligned with one of the PhD papers, this Master's thesis can still help the PhD student to accelerate their literature review for the respective paper, for instance. Meanwhile, the Master's student will benefit from a supervisor that is particularly invested in the Master's thesis – after all, the supervisor needs a thorough literature review which requires several rounds of feedback to aid the completion of the PhD paper.

Working intensely with undergraduate and graduate students throughout a PhD can be a zero-cost method for the PhD student to support the PhD start-up. If you can access multiple students, you may even want to choose to test more risky research ideas via these students. For instance, you could propose that a graduate student writes their Master's thesis on a topic for which you are not entirely sure if it will be possible to collect original data. You support the Master's student as much as possible throughout their thesis – and you ensure upfront that a respectable thesis could also be written only based on secondary data (which is usually possible for Master's theses). If the student manages to overcome the challenges associated with your proposed research, you continue to pursue this idea and potentially turn it into a great paper. If the anticipated challenges materialize, you drop the idea. You then invested fewer resources into it than you would have done if attempting to implement it without a Master's student.

Even if you are unable to work with students, you may be able to try out riskier research ideas with limited investment of resources. Digital technology has radically slashed data collection costs for many social scientists. This may hold particularly true for scientists who embrace qualitative methods. Most qualitative researchers are reported to prefer face-to-face interviews to telephone interviews because they supposedly lead to more insightful data.[150] I also believe in the relevance of fieldwork. I met a scholar during my time in Oxford who had written a book about Myanmar without ever having visited the country. This is absurd.

However, fieldwork can also be extremely expensive. For instance, a night in a hostel in Yangon, Myanmar, can cost GBP 40. The scholar spending a month in Yangon spends GBP 1,200 on accommodation alone. Hence, it may be advisable for any cost-conscious scholar to combine fieldwork with digital technologies. Scholars found 25 years ago that there were 'no remarkable differences' between information collected via telephone and information collected via face-to-face interviews.[151] More recent research has particularly advocated video telephony via Skype as a suitable equivalent to face-to-face interviews for those who lack financial resources for carrying out extended periods of field research.[152]

All the initial interviews I carried out for my dissertation were via Skype. The intention of these was to gauge if it would be possible to interview Chinese dam developers, a group I was hoping to focus several papers on at the beginning of my doctorate. I could have flown to South East Asia for these initial interviews, spending GBP 1,000 just for the flights. Instead, I spent no financial resources on interviewing in the beginning and only headed to South East Asia once I had established a sufficient network via Skype interviews. This network ensured that I could access Chinese dam developers (comparatively) promptly once I had arrived.

Choices that favour digital technologies need to be defended at times, since many scholars remain sceptical of the possibilities attached to them – including those of mainstream technologies like Skype. For instance, one reviewer of one of my papers complained that many of my interviews 'were telephone interviews or online surveys/email exchange'. I responded that 'empirical research has found [...] that just as much insightful information can be collected via telephone interviews as can be via face-to-face interviews'. The point was not raised again.

▶ 3.5 On rapid conference iteration

Founders of start-ups who adhere to the lean start-up approach are usually keen to spend a lot of time pitching their ideas at start-up conferences. 'These are ideal occasions to collect feedback on your business model', a founder once told me. Admission to these conferences is often competitive, with hundreds of start-ups applying for only a few pitch slots. For instance, more than 300 applications were collected for only 15 pitch spots at a recent start-up conference in Berlin. The application was lean, though. 'Tell us about your business model and the current stage of your start-up (four to five sentences) or send us a short pitch deck!' the organizers wrote.[153] Those admitted could pitch their business plan via a three-minute-presentation in front of an audience of 400 people – from angel investors to corporations, journalists and policy-makers. If the business model is already convincing, funding can directly develop out of such pitches.

There are similarities between conferences for start-ups and academic conferences. First, admission to both types of conferences is usually competitive. For instance, only 28 per cent of applications to the annual conference of the Association for Computational Linguistics (ACL), a research society for people working on problems involving natural language and computation, were accepted in 2016.[154] Furthermore, the amount of information required to apply for an academic conference is (surprisingly) almost as minimal as for start-up conferences. Most academic conference organizers only ask for an abstract of 150 to 250 words that outlines the research that scholars wish to present. However, many PhDs still do not apply to academic conferences, while start-up founders are extremely keen to attend conferences. Indeed, those organizing academic conferences often only receive a handful of applications from PhD students even if hundreds of presentation slots are to be filled.

Many PhD students do not apply for conferences since they fear being critiqued for their work. Indeed, I know many PhD students who only present their work at conferences after many months (and sometimes years) of work because of this. Admittedly, conference feedback can be harsh, although usually not as harsh as anonymous feedback provided by journal reviewers – it is anonymity that can bring out the worst in academics.[155] I still recall, though, how I once attended a conference at St Antony's College, University of Oxford, where I was verbally slaughtered by the audience for suggesting that large dams may be part of Myanmar's future energy mix. That was an unpleasant experience.

Retrospectively, however, the experience was helpful. The audience raised arguments that I had not considered previously and this helped me to further refine my thinking on my topic. I presented the same research again at a conference a few months later with my presentation now incorporating the previous audience's comments – and the new audience was suddenly much more positive regarding my work. The different conference comments I gathered were also reflected in the dissertation I finally submitted.

I argued earlier in this chapter that the end user of the execution phase of the lean PhD is the peer reviewer of an academic journal. Publishing in prestigious academic journals is what this phase is all about. Scholars in your field decide about your publication in these journals and these scholars are attending conference after conference to find their next collaborators, to broaden their horizons, to develop new research ideas or just to collect feedback from colleagues on their current work.

The PhD student embracing lean methodologies also attends conferences to collect feedback from colleagues. This does not only help you to directly improve your thinking on a topic. If you receive only a little critical feedback on your work at a conference, this can also be an indicator that your paper is ready to be submitted to a journal. If you are stuck with your paper, conference feedback may be just what you need to unstick yourself. There are also tactical reasons for attending academic conferences. If conference feedback is incorporated and a colleague whose feedback you incorporated in your work then reviews it for a journal, they will be much more likely to judge it favourably. Furthermore, it usually helps if you met (and socialized) with those that review your work. It is much more difficult to reject the work of someone who you started befriending than someone who you have never encountered. I presented my work at 15 conferences throughout my PhD and I suggest to any PhD student that they should attend at least as many. It can only boost the academic quality and impact of your work. Once some initial data has been collected, you are good to go to an academic conference.

> ### Try this ... for rapid conference iteration
>
> - Present your work at conferences once you have a rough idea of what you are doing
> - Note down and then incorporate all feedback you collect at conferences
> - Socialize with those that are likely to review your work

Conferences which mix practitioners and academics can also be a fantastic opportunity for your work. One of the first conferences I attended during my PhD was HYDRO 2015, which brings together dam developers, policy-makers and (a few) academics from all around the world. This conference helped me to connect with hydropower players that would not respond to any of my previous reach-outs. Interviewing these players at the conference helped to improve my work. Furthermore, audience feedback from this conference helped me to write my work in a way that was more accessible to stakeholders from the industry – key for the practical impact of my work. One more example of the value of conferences with practitioners: I was recently approached by a journalist after a presentation at Stockholm World Water Week who asked if I wanted to write a commentary on my research topic, based on my presentation. Such commentaries are a great tool to boost the visibility of your research beyond academic circles. I further discuss this in Chapter 4 of this book.

Both the PhD student who is on a paper route and the one who is writing a traditional thesis are well-advised to attend conferences. While the PhD student on a paper route will present their most recent draft paper, the traditional thesis PhD student may choose to present a chapter they are currently working on. Since thesis chapters tend to be more integrated into the entire dissertation than papers, the PhD student presenting a thesis chapter may need to provide more context upfront to ensure the audience can contribute helpful feedback on their work.

Admittedly, conferences featuring practitioners, in particular, can be costly to attend. Prohibitive costs may also be a major reason for the small numbers of applications filed by PhD students for academic conferences. I recently attended the 24th conference of the International Sustainable Development Research Society, a large event on sustainable development research. Scholars from the United Kingdom had to pay a registration fee of GBP 530 to attend this conference. Add GBP 850 for flights (the conference was held in Colombia), GBP 300 for the Airbnb and GBP 100 for miscellaneous items such as in-transit Wi-Fi. The costs are roughly equal to the monthly net salary of a postdoctoral student in the UK.[156]

Conferences used to be more affordable. However, many have grown fancier over the years. While conferences have been held in universities for hundreds of years, many are now hosted in expensive hotels or conference centres. For instance, the last annual meeting of the American Association of Geographers, the world's largest geography conference, was in the Sheraton Boston, a four-star venue. Many academic conferences now also feature elaborate social programmes. Those who attend Stockholm World Water Week must choose whether the cocktail reception on Monday night, the royal banquet on Wednesday night or the 'mingle and dance' on Thursday night is the conference's main see-and-be-seen event.[156]

Fixing academic conferences is not rocket science, as I recently wrote in *The Guardian* in what some friends called 'an angry commentary'.[156] Most early career scholars would likely welcome it if future conferences were hosted in universities instead of four-star hotels. I suspect that very few would protest if cocktail receptions, banquets and dance nights were dropped to invest more in conference grants. The next generation of scholars would probably also not mind if parts of conferences went virtual. Slowly, academics have started experimenting with the current conference format. For instance, the Feminist and Women's Studies Association of the UK and Ireland recently held a conference that was entirely virtual – a very cost-efficient set-up that is conducive for PhD students. Many more of these initiatives are needed, though. Otherwise, rapid conference iterations – the key idea of this section of the book – remain the privilege of well-funded PhD students.

Those PhD students who cannot attend (m)any academic conferences may be encouraged by reading that numerous academic conferences do not deliver on their promises. For instance, I was at several conferences where I received zero comments on my work afterwards. I also had the impression that at least three-quarters of the audience was not listening to what I presented. This is of little surprise when you present in the late afternoon of a conference day and attendees have listened to often dozens of 15-minute presentations prior to yours. Such conferences are of limited help to boost the quality of your work via insightful feedback. I now ask around regarding the usefulness of conferences prior to attending any and I also recommend that my PhD students research the quality of any academic conference prior to submitting an abstract to it.

Insights from a PhD researcher

I am pursuing my research as an external PhD student. This means that I am not working on my research as part of a group in a university, but that I work independently from home. Hence, I have far fewer options to bounce ideas with PhD students and other researchers than others do. Workshops and conferences are thus particularly important for me to advance in my work. I have attended two workshops this year to collect feedback on my work. I was particularly keen on feedback on the method I employ, qualitative content analysis, since my supervisor is not so familiar with this method. The inputs gathered during both workshops proved to be very helpful to me. However, I will think even more closely about what I want to get out of this kind of iteration before the next workshop or conference that I attend. The more precise questions you ask your audience when closing your presentation, the more helpful the answers will be, according to my experience. I would really recommend to any PhD student to attend as many conferences and workshops as possible to collect feedback on your work. This is an efficient way to advance your research, while boosting its quality, visibility and thus also its potential impact.

Claudia Regler, PhD Student (Political Science), University of Münster, Germany

▶ **3.6 Pivoting**

I briefly mentioned the term 'pivoting' in Chapter 2 of this book. While it is not at the very core of the lean start-up approach, it is an essential element of it which can be of particular relevance for those adhering to the lean approach when executing a PhD. A pivot, within the lean methodologies, is changing the plan instead of the person executing it. Pivoting can result from multiple attempts of rapid prototyping that did not lead to any encouraging feedback from end users. The start-up founder then fundamentally changes their core business idea instead of changing their team (or giving up founding), which would be the traditional approach in launching a company.

There are numerous examples of successful start-up pivots. One of the most famous ones in recent years may be Twitter. Twitter started out as a company called Odeo, a network where people could find and subscribe to podcasts. When iTunes began taking over the podcast niche, the company's founders feared that Odeo would not be able to survive this competition. Odeo's employees were then given two weeks to come up with a fundamentally new idea for the start-up's business model. The idea embraced by Odeo's founder was that of a status-updating micro-blogging platform. This was the birth of Twitter.[157] Twitter now counts around 330 million users worldwide.[158]

Admittedly, companies were pivoting even before the term was coined. Another famous example of pivoting is Starbucks. The company started out in 1971 as a firm selling espresso makers and coffee beans and it did not create much buzz while doing so. Howard Schultz, Starbucks' current chairman, president and chief executive officer (CEO), found upon a visit of coffee houses in Italy in 1983 that brewing and selling coffee could be a more promising endeavour. He thus decided to switch Starbucks' business model, and Starbucks as a European-style coffee shop was born.[157] Starbucks now operates more than 25,000 stores in 75 countries worldwide.[159]

Many PhD students will stick to their topic even if gathering meaningful results on it has failed again and again: the idea of pivoting is foreign to them, according to my experience. Instead, these students drop out of the PhD. They blame themselves for their lack of progress. However, following the lean PhD approach, students should not question their ability to conduct research when their PhD endeavour does not progress. Rather, such stagnation (first) calls into question whether the topic is suitable for further investigation. The lean PhD student simply changes the plan instead of firing the one executing it. Quitting the PhD is an option (and I discuss this further at the end of Chapter 4), but it is the option of last resort. Changing the topic of the PhD is the first route to consider.

Try this ... for pivoting

- Go 'all in' for your chosen research topic
- Switch your topic once you are reasonably certain that it is a dead end
- Recycle as much of your previous work as possible in your new topic

---

Changing one's research topic is a difficult decision to make. Much work has likely been invested in this topic already. This work has already been incurred and cannot be recovered. It is 'sunk costs', as a consultant would say. Questions to ask when considering a pivot are: will my current topic yield enough results to justify the award of a PhD? Is there another topic that I find interesting enough to pursue a PhD on? How much more time will I likely need to invest to complete a PhD on this alternative topic? Can I finance this time? Could my current supervisor still work with me if I change course? Who could be alternative supervisors?

Pivoting sounds scary, but it can be the key to completing a PhD efficiently, while delivering high-quality and impactful work. I pivoted 11 months into my PhD and still submitted my PhD 21 months after starting it. I outlined earlier that my initial research proposal was on the socio-economic impacts of large dams. Only upon commencing my PhD did I realize that scholars had been working on this topic since the late 1950s (admittedly, if my research proposal had not been so lean, I may have realized this earlier). The more time I spent on my literature review in the first few months of my PhD, the more excellent studies I found on my topic. A key criterion for obtaining a PhD is to find out something novel, as outlined in Chapter 1. I realized that this would be difficult in my chosen field, given the breadth and depth of research at hand. Nevertheless, I stuck to my initial field, identifying (one-by-one) numerous niches within it that provided the potential for a contribution via additional research on them.

The PhD at the University of Oxford is organized in a stage-gate model. This is an excellent model for organizing a PhD and from my point of view one which needs to be copied by many universities. Its key advantage is that it provides thorough feedback to the PhD student along the entire PhD endeavour. It is thus one that resonates with the lean start-up methodologies. Several examinations are undertaken as milestones within this model. The PhD student must pass each of these milestones to continue their research at the university and only once all milestones are passed are they able to submit the dissertation. The first milestone is the transfer-of-status examination which determines that the student is developing a convincing research proposal.[160] I completed my transfer-of-status report six months after enrolling at the university and I received feedback from my assessors five months after that.

Both assessors challenged my report. My first assessor wrote:

> The candidate has identified four clear niches in the literature of social impacts of dams. If successful, it will yield four worthwhile papers. I wonder, however, whether the targeting of niches somehow lacks ambition to take on the 'big issues' of social impacts of dams. The author argues that these are already well-researched, which is true, but also hints at the possibility for original thinking within this mature literature. I encourage the candidate to consider that challenge.

I agreed with the assessor's point, and I decided to consider the challenge he posed. However, I could not find any coherent contribution in my original literature field even after weeks and weeks of thinking about it. Hence I responded to the assessors' comments by proposing to change the very topic of my research. I suggested switching the focus from dams' social impacts to anti-dam movements. These are very different literatures. The first one is dominated by anthropologists, the second one is grounded mostly in sociology. While much has been written in this first literature, anti-dam movements, until today, have been barely explored by scholars. I thus saw myriad possibilities for a coherent contribution to this field.

My transfer-of-status examination took place in the eleventh month of my PhD. I had conducted dozens of interviews by then. I had even submitted papers from my work to journals. In sum, I had spent a substantial amount of time on my first research topic. Nevertheless, I presented my novel topic and the rationale for this topic to my assessors since this seemed to me the most straightforward path to efficiently completing a high-quality and impactful PhD. Both found my new proposal convincing. They encouraged me to think about how to leverage as much as possible from my previous work in my new work, which I did. And so I completely changed my topic 10 months into the PhD and yet I submitted my entire PhD 11 months later.

4 Exiting the PhD

This chapter explains:

- Why the minimum viable dissertation (MVD) is all that is needed to complete a PhD
- How to strategically choose examiners
- Why it makes sense to aim for revisions
- Why and how to go the extra mile for the lean PhD
- How to boost the practical impact of your PhD
- When to quit your PhD

▶ 4.1 The minimum viable dissertation

While many start-up founders claim to be wanting to change the world with their enterprise,[161] survey data on start-up founders suggests that this is not their main motivation when launching a start-up. Rather, the most commonly named motivation is 'the desire to build wealth'. Seventy-five per cent of start-up founders list this as their key motivation in one recent survey.[162] This aim is achieved via what in the start-up universe is called an 'exit'. A popular exit option is the initial public offering (IPO) where the founder sells a part of their business to the public in the form of shares.[163] An alternative to an IPO is an acquisition of the start-up by a larger firm.[163] For instance, the start-up Cardioxyl Pharmaceuticals, a company founded in 2005 which works on therapies to treat heart diseases, was acquired for USD 2.1 billion by Bristol-Myers Squibb, a large American pharmaceutical company, in one of 2015's largest start-up exits.[164]

Start-ups do not need a perfect business model for a successful IPO. A famous example for this is Twitter. Twitter's IPO took place in 2013. The firm raised USD 1.8 billion through the sale of 70 million shares (with a price of USD 26 per share) via its IPO. However, the company was not profitable at the time of the IPO. While it reported revenues of USD 422 million for the first nine months of 2013, it still faced losses of USD 134 for the same period.[165] Twitter is a success according to some dimensions. It is said to have played a critical role in the 2011 Arab Spring as well as in the election of a political outsider, Donald Trump, as president of the United States.[166] It may thus be 'one of the most powerful [political] forces on the planet, for better, and sometimes worse' as digitalization thought leader Bruce Judson writes.[166] Twitter's IPO turned at least 16 people from its team into millionaires and billionaires.[167] However, 12 years after its founding, Twitter is not even close to making money and many are unsure that it will ever turn a profit.[168]

Obtaining a doctorate is the exit for the PhD student. Just as start-ups do not need a perfect business model for their exit, PhD students do not need a perfect dissertation to obtain this doctorate. The PhD does not have to be a masterpiece.[169] All that is needed is a decent dissertation. However, this view is not propagated much in contemporary academia. Rather, many supervisors cultivate the ideal that any dissertation must be a significant piece of work that has vastly enhanced mankind's understanding of a specific problem with several policy implications derivable from it. Some even create the impression that a PhD thesis ought to achieve nothing less than saving the world.[170] This kind of narrative then fosters a perfectionism that can be paralysing for the PhD student.[169]

The truth is that very few researchers achieve fame because of their dissertation.[171] Consider the example of star economist Jeffrey Sachs (about whom I will write more later in this chapter). He completed his PhD at Harvard University in 1980. It was entitled 'Factor Costs and Macroeconomic Adjustment in the Open Economy: Theory and Evidence'.[172] Sachs numbers more than 105,000 citations, according to Google Scholar, with citations being widely accepted as the main operationalization of academic impact. His PhD thesis has not contributed a single citation to this count.[173] Sachs has been dubbed 'the world's best-known economist'.[174] Yet his thesis has had zero academic impact.

It is of little surprise that most PhDs go unnoticed. After all, the PhD is usually one's very first attempt at carrying out a piece of original research. The gifted painter will not paint a portrait of the calibre of the *Mona Lisa* when delivering their first piece of work. Similarly, the PhD student will not write a work of the calibre of Karl Marx's *Das Kapital* (which is the most cited book in the social sciences published before 1950, according to one analysis[175]) when delivering their PhD thesis. Academic writing is a skill and this skill takes many years to hone. Even an academic wunderkind such as Jeffrey Sachs apparently did not have it when completing his doctorate.

When I completed my doctorate, I aimed for what I call a 'minimum viable dissertation' (MVD). This dissertation is just good enough to receive a doctorate. It is not a masterwork and it does not want to be one. In fact, some parts of the MVD may and should not be particularly compelling. I very much believe that adopting the MVD as one's aim for a dissertation can be a great accelerator for any PhD endeavour, while also significantly boosting one's well-being. I already outlined in Chapter 1 that half of all PhD students suffer from psychological distress. Perfectionism has been repeatedly recognized as a major cause for such distress.[176-178] The MVD approach emancipates the PhD student from this perfectionism that is rife in academia and replaces it with the pragmatism that is characteristic for successful start-up founders.

Sadly, pragmatism is lacking in most of the academy and it is thus also rarely found in the guidelines of PhD requirements. Indeed, even PhDs that are written via the 'paper route' that I recommended in Chapter 2 do not only consist of papers. Rather, the papers must be embedded in what I call a 'coat'. This coat needs to be between 15,000 and 20,000 words at Oxford University's School of Geography and the Environment where I completed my PhD. It includes an introduction, a literature review, a chapter on methodology and a conclusion. Those in the academy usually confess that this coat (with the exception being the conclusion part) is barely read by anyone besides your supervisors and the assessors of your thesis.

Try this ... for the minimum viable dissertation (MVD)

- Write at least one outstanding chapter and/or paper for your dissertation
- Write the 'coat' of your dissertation (the introduction, literature review, methods section and conclusion) as quickly as possible
- Submit your dissertation once every part of it is at least 'good enough'

This implies that very little time should be spent on creating the coat, whereas this advice is frequently not followed in the academy. Indeed, I know of one student who spent more than a year on creating the coat of his thesis.[96] Meanwhile, I set myself a deadline of not taking any longer than five working days for any chapter of the coat, i.e. I wrote my introductory chapter in a week, I wrote my literature review in a week and so on. It seemed (and it still seems) unreasonable to me to spend any longer on a piece of work that remains largely unnoticed and I hope that more and more universities will start allowing paper-based PhDs that only consist of the actual papers, a brief introduction and a conclusion that summarizes the core argument of the student's work. (This type of PhD is already allowed at the university I now work at, Utrecht University.)

A coat that is good enough must still fulfil various basic requirements. For instance, the introduction must outline the academic and societal relevance of the PhD student's work. Meanwhile, the literature review must demonstrate the PhD student's understanding of the relevant field of study and the methods section must succinctly justify why the PhD student chose which methods for their work. If a PhD student delivers an introduction, literature review or methods section that is substandard, this can lead and has led to much more than major revisions in the viva, as also noted by a reviewer of this book.

While I very much believe that the coat of the PhD thesis can and should be no more than barely good enough (and while I acknowledge that the coat is not something that exists in PhD theses in the arts and humanities), this does not mean that the entire dissertation can or should be. Indeed, a dissertation that is barely good enough from the first to the last page will only pass at very few universities around the world. Any dissertation needs to contain promising threads and materials that excite the assessors for the doctorate. There needs to be some evident contribution. This, for instance, can be one paper that is part of the paper-based PhD. It is common knowledge in the academy that a single outstanding paper can make a career for any scientist. Similarly, a single interesting paper can suffice for a PhD to be awarded. I will further discuss in Section 4.4 how PhD students can signal to assessors that their work contains a contribution.

Your supervisors usually need to endorse your submission of your dissertation. It can be difficult to obtain this endorsement if the coat of your thesis is only good enough, in combination with your supervisors not embracing the lean PhD approach. I never explicitly negotiated with my supervisors the quality standard of my dissertation's coat. Instead, I just shared with them the quality that I could achieve in a chapter after five days of work (which was not very impressive). Sometimes my supervisors would give their 'Okay' to this quality, sometimes I was asked to undertake major revisions. Overall, my supervisors gave their 'Okay' more often than major revisions. More on this also in Section 4.4.

▶ 4.2 Strategically choosing examiners

Successful start-up founders in the exiting phase of their endeavour can be choosy. If the founder goes for an exit by acquisition, several firms may be keen to acquire the start-up founder's firm. The founder can then significantly influence the exit conditions. If the founder is to stay with the company upon the exit, the founder may choose the acquiring firm with the culture that they believe they particularly click with. The founder may also go for the firm whose business model is believed to be most synergetic with their start-up since this raises the chances for the start-up's scaling (which can further boost the start-up founder's acquisition bonus[179]).

Similarly, the PhD student can be choosy regarding their exit. Most countries require the first supervisor of the PhD student to choose the PhD student's assessors. The supervisor is the PhD student's core ally in the lean PhD – and ideally also in any other type of PhD. Some countries such as the Netherlands require up to five external assessors for a single PhD. German universities usually only require a single external assessor, with the PhD student's supervisor acting as the dissertation's internal assessor. Meanwhile, the University of Oxford requires one external assessor and one internal assessor (and the internal assessor cannot be the PhD student's supervisor).

I discussed in Chapter 3 how the peer-review process can be almost as random as a coin toss. The assessment of the PhD student's thesis is also a peer review. However, the randomness of this peer review can be minimized since the assessors can be chosen, whereas those reviewing one's work submitted to a journal are (ideally) impossible to influence. Being able to choose one's examiners (via one's supervisor) can be advantageous for at least two reasons. First, a PhD student can choose an examiner that they click with – which enhances the chances of a hitch-free viva. Second, the PhD student can choose an examiner whose work prepared the ground for the PhD student's work. Any examiner will be flattered by a dissertation that is advancing their scholarship.

Try this ... for strategically choosing examiners

- Discuss potential examiners as early as possible with your supervisor
- Go for examiners that you click with
- In addition, go for those whose work yours builds on

I knew both my internal and external examiner for my viva. I knew my internal examiner already from my confirmation-of-status examination and multiple departmental roundtables and talks. I was not entirely sure that I clicked with him, but my first-choice internal examiner (with whom I believed I clicked and who had already assessed my work during my transfer-of-status and confirmation-of-status examinations) argued that his subject expertise would be too distant from my thesis to thoroughly assess it, so a substitute was needed.

Meanwhile, I had interviewed my external examiner as an expert during the first few months of my doctorate and felt that there was a personal fit.

Most importantly, though, much of my work directly built upon my external examiner's research. For instance, the entire fourth and final paper of my doctorate was based on a framework he had developed. Overall, his works were probably the ones I cited most in my entire thesis. I was thus optimistic that he would read my thesis with great interest and would also be appreciative of it, although I departed methodologically from his approaches at times. While my internal examiner had not carried out any work on my topic and I could thus not base any of my scholarly writing on his work (nobody in my department carried out work on my topic before I arrived), I knew that he was sympathetic to one of my work's key messages (which was 'Chinese dam developers are not as malicious as claimed by the popular press') and I thus deemed him to be a decent fit.

My supervisor asked me who I considered would be suitable assessors for my thesis which allowed me to choose examiners with whom I knew I shared a common outlook. However, even PhD students who are unable to do so can still influence the outcome of their viva. Most importantly, having papers from the dissertation published helps to ensure a hitch-free viva. A rule of thumb that is frequently shared in my current department at Utrecht University is that no assessors will fail a PhD if two papers out of it have been accepted by peer-reviewed journals already. These papers do not even have to be accepted by the most prestigious journals. Indeed, having papers accepted in any peer-reviewed journal is already a notable accomplishment for any PhD student.

Second, already having lined up the next stage regarding one's career at the time of the viva helps. I started my PhD in January 2015 and submitted it in September 2016, as I have outlined. My defence was scheduled for November 2016. Many defences will be scheduled three to four months after completion of the thesis since assessors often demand so much time for reading it. I was appointed as an assistant professor by Utrecht University in October 2016 with my work supposed to start in January 2017. At least my internal assessor knew about this at the time of the viva – and he also knew that demanding significant revisions could significantly hamper my start in my new job. While assessors may be particularly sympathetic to those that stay in the academy (and will thus not pose major obstacles to them via significant revisions), only a few will obstruct you via significant revisions (or even worse) if you have lined up a job outside of the academy. However, if you have no evident plan yet at the time of the viva, some assessors may be tempted to push you to further hone the quality of your dissertation. And there will always be issues to improve on.

> ### Insights from a PhD researcher
>
> I pursued my PhD at Oxford University's Department of Physics, studying evolutionary biology by using tools from theoretical computer science. When I approached the end of my PhD, I chose my examiners very carefully. I had to pick someone from inside the university, and someone from outside. Considering I was the only student in the whole university studying my topic, finding a suitable assessor at Oxford University became quite a challenge. Furthermore, I was involved in a paper with many of my supervisor's collaborators from other universities, which also made it difficult to find someone from outside who was not already a part of this collaboration (which rendered them ineligible). Eventually, I decided to choose my examiners based on how my thesis resonated with the general direction of their work. While there are many evolutionary biologists at Oxford University, most of them are very unfamiliar with my approach, which I feared would result in a series of off-topic questions coming from frustrated examiners. Instead, I chose a computer scientist as my internal and a mathematician as my external examiner, with both having published a few papers on evolution. I thus thought that they would be familiar both with my approach and my topic and this proved to be true. Overall, I urge any PhD student to think strategically about choosing examiners. Wise choices regarding examiners can really simplify your defence a lot.
>
> **Chico Camargo, Postdoctoral Researcher (Physics), University of Oxford, United Kingdom**

▶ 4.3 Aiming for revisions

For many entrepreneurs, it is the exit that they dream about.[180] While the exit may turn a start-up founder into a millionaire, their journey does not end with the exit. Indeed, many founders stay with their firms after the exit – and some even have to do so since this is negotiated as an exit condition. An example of this is the acquisition of the start-up GrandCentral, a phone management service that eventually became Google Voice,[181] by Google for USD 60 million in 2007. As part of the exit deal, GrandCentral's founder Craig Walker agreed to stay with his firm for another two years – and he ended up staying even longer than that because he apparently liked it so much at Google.[180] Investors often ask founders to stay since founders hold the most knowledge on their start-up and it may thus be difficult to steer the company without them.

Just as the start-up founder's journey does not end with the exit, the PhD student's journey does not end with obtaining the doctorate. Rather, the doctorate is a stepping stone to the next steps in the PhD student's career, which can be inside or outside of academia. However, it is not always seen as such by PhD students, particularly if the PhD journey has been an unpleasant one. Indeed, many PhD students who have spent a number of years of their lives on their PhD often hope that this chapter will end with their dissertation defence. The defence is to immediately result in the doctorate and it is then hoped that one must never think about the PhD again.

Yet the student who believes their PhD will end with the dissertation defence confuses the dissertation with the PhD. The dissertation is only a subset of the PhD – a conceptualization which also resonates with current discussions regarding PhDs in the United Kingdom. Various research councils and quality assurance agencies have repeatedly highlighted, as also noted by one of the reviewers of this book, that the PhD is to be understood as the process of training a researcher, while the thesis is considered as the core output of this training. The process of training a researcher starts many years prior to the submission of the dissertation and this process may never be completed.

The perception that the submission of the dissertation is the end of the PhD process can create a lot of unnecessary work. The PhD student who wants to finish their doctorate with the PhD defence will try to deliver a thesis as perfect as possible in order not to receive any revisions and thus be able to leave the PhD behind. Many PhD students even perceive revisions as almost failing the PhD. This is bogus. While revisions are rather rare in some countries, e.g. Germany or the Netherlands, they are common in others. For instance, four out of five PhD students in the United Kingdom receive revisions.[7]

I aimed for revisions when submitting my dissertation and I recommend that any PhD student does the same. The idea of aiming for revisions is grounded in the lean start-up principles. I outlined in Chapter 1 that the lean start-up approach is all about confronting the end user with a minimum viable product as soon as possible with the intention to then introduce targeted improvements to the product via the end user's feedback. The end users in the exiting phase of the PhD are the assessors of your dissertation. The lean start-up approach suggests seeking their feedback on your work as soon as possible. The assessors are your allies in the PhD process if you adopt the lean start-up approach. It is their task to help you sharpen your thesis. But you need their comments on your work to be able to be as targeted as possible in any improvements you undertake.

Try this ... when aiming for revisions

- Do not consider the viva as the very end of your PhD
- Your examiners are your allies
- Discuss your viva revisions with your supervisor(s)

Another reason to aim for revisions is the imperfection of the peer-review process. I outlined in Chapter 3 that peer review can be as random as a coin toss, with several studies finding that reviewers frequently do not agree in their evaluations of a specific manuscript. While you can somewhat manage the comments you will receive from your assessors by strategically choosing these assessors, it is almost impossible to entirely guess your assessors' comments upfront. Those who undertake one round of preemptive revisions after the other with the intention of delivering a seemingly perfect thesis are thus wasting a lot of time.

You would expect that your assessors at least detect any major methodological errors in your thesis. Sadly, research suggests otherwise. A study published in the *Journal of the Royal Society of Medicine* illustrates this. Three test papers were sent to 607 peer reviewers from the *British Medical Journal*, one of the world's oldest medical journals, for this study. Each of the papers contained nine major methodological errors. One would hope that reviewers detected every single one of these errors. However, reviewers found no more than three on average. The reviewers' error detection did not even improve significantly when they received a short training session on error detection.[182] This suggests that your assessors may oversee major errors in your work, while many other comments they provide may be purely based on their taste. Even outstanding dissertations may receive major revisions, given the unreliability of the peer-review process.

Pursuing my PhD in the United Kingdom, there was an 80 per cent chance that I would receive revisions. Indeed, it seems like the very task of assessors in the United Kingdom is to provide the PhD students with revisions. Two of the four papers in the core of my thesis were already published by the time I submitted it and my assessors were thus not able to provide many comments on these papers since anything that successfully undergoes peer review is viewed to be final in the academy. At the same time, the coat of my thesis was what I considered to be barely good enough, and thus an invitation to my assessors to provide many comments. This is also what happened with the two first sentences of the suggested revisions for my dissertation, which read: 'The examiners agreed that the thesis contains excellent materials. They also agreed that the main problem lies in the framing [which is the coat] of the core chapters, all of which are presented as standalone papers.'

My assessors asked me to undertake major revisions upon my PhD defence. In concrete terms, I was asked to undertake 45 different amendments to my work before my PhD was granted. Most of these were very specific requests, though. For instance, one read 'p. 53: Sentence starting "I believe" unclear'. Another one read: 'p. 179, bottom line: What is meant by "medics"?'. While it took my university about two months to share the different requested amendments with me, it was a mere three days of work to then incorporate the required changes.

I resubmitted the thesis after my supervisors had also examined the various changes I had undertaken (your supervisors' experience can be a great asset here), and my doctorate was then approved.

A final comment on the PhD defence: while I encourage aiming for revisions, this does not imply that the viva ought to be taken lightly. The viva is not just another round of feedback. If it is conceptualized as such, the risk will be great that you are asked to undertake much more than the few tweaks. After all, your assessors will consider the viva as the grand finale of your PhD process and you need to play along with this if you do not want to fail. I discuss in the next section how you can signal that you also see the viva as the grand finale of your PhD process.

▶ 4.4 Going the extra mile

I already outlined in Chapter 1 that start-up founders work extremely hard. On average, a start-up entrepreneur invests 55 hours to 100 hours per week in their endeavour.[183] The lean start-up approach can help to reduce the hours needed per week, while ensuring that efforts are more targeted. Nevertheless, founding a successful company will likely always require blood, sweat and tears, as outlined earlier. 'There is no easy path to success', a typical start-up saying goes.

Like the lean start-up approach, the lean PhD approach outlined in this book can significantly reduce the time you need for completing a PhD. I estimated earlier that it may halve it, given that I submitted my PhD in 45 per cent of the average time needed before submission at my university. However, if your PhD seems to your supervisors and assessors like one that is rushed, you will most likely run into problems. After all, slowness is a central value in academia and it is linked to quality.[184,185] Indeed, the belief that quality is a function of time is omnipresent. The more time you invest, the greater your work's quality will be, goes the common belief.

The upholding of slowness as a virtue is fostered by the tenure system. In 2013, the jobs website CareerCast named university professor as the number one least stressful job in the world.[186] It is certainly the least stressful job that I have ever had. A professor has no boss. No one keeps track of a professor's activities or whereabouts. No one intervenes when the professor needs four months instead of four days to provide feedback on a paper by their PhD student.[187] No one can rush a professor and this often also spills over to the professor's team where nobody is rushing.

Conceptualizing quality as an outcome of time is worthwhile. Questions investigated by academics are complex and thus much time is required to think them through. However, contemporary academia all too frequently emphasizes quantity over quality. As scholars Maggie Berg and Barbara Seeber write: 'You [the contemporary academic system] want [us] to pump out as much stuff as quickly as [possible]. That's going to have consequences for how thoughtful things are.'[185] If there is one sector that must be cultivating deep thought, it is the academic one and it frequently still does that.[186]

However, presenting quality as an outcome of slowness can also be problematic at times. For instance, the first one to complete a mathematics exam in high school was often also the one that would obtain the highest mark in the class. Meanwhile, the students who completed the exam last were frequently the ones who failed. I observed a similar correlation while working in consulting. I interviewed candidates who wanted to join my company by posing case studies to them, among other things. These usually contained some calculations. Some candidates were immediately able to carry out these calculations. Others struggled. However, if I provided more time to this second group, even if I provided much more time, these candidates would usually not find a solution after five or more minutes either. If I gave them another calculation to complete, they would struggle just as much. Taking a lot of time for something can also be an indication that one is not particularly good at it.

Opening this kind of discussion likely does not help you in passing your PhD defence, though. The idea that haste makes waste is just too dominant in contemporary academia. Hence, you need to signal that your PhD is not a rushed submission if you submit it after two years instead of the four years that may be the average duration of a PhD at your institution. If the PhD comes across as quick and dirty work (which is a significant risk especially if it has been submitted very rapidly), rejection is almost certain. As we have seen, Marissa Mayer does not invest in start-up founders that do not work at least 130 hours per week.[183] Similarly, most professors will not allow a PhD student to pass if no evidence is provided that the work undertaken was worthwhile. The PhD dissertation that is submitted after two years (or even earlier) thus needs to be one that is 'overdue'. There cannot be a single sign of rushing through.

I chose two options to signal that my PhD was not a rushed one. The first relates to the data I collected. My doctoral work was mostly qualitative. Thirty-one qualitative interviews are conducted in total on average for a qualitative PhD.[189] The largest sample size that was found in an analysis of 2,433 qualitative PhD dissertations was 95.[189] If you download my PhD dissertation, you will find a table in its Chapter 3 that lists 131 interviews. These are all interviews that I conducted for my PhD – 38 per cent more than in the largest qualitative PhD from a sample size perspective, as identified in the cited study. I mentioned several times throughout my defence how the size of my dataset compares with other qualitative PhDs. I also pointed out that I thus collected the largest dataset ever assembled on my PhD topic (which was possible due to the tremendous help of undergraduate students, as discussed in Chapter 3). While I may have come across as somewhat annoying, I also believe that this helped to signal that my PhD was thorough, instead of rushed.

Try this ... when going the extra mile

- Collect the largest dataset ever collected on your topic
- Alternatively, significantly improve a specific method for your PhD, or create that grand theory the world has been waiting for
- Have at least one paper/chapter out of your PhD published by the time of your viva

---

Developing and analysing a particularly large dataset is one kind of contribution, an empirical contribution, that can justify awarding a PhD. Another kind of contribution is a methodological one. A methodological contribution implies that you further developed a particular research method in your PhD (or you may even have developed a completely novel research method from scratch). A third kind of contribution is the theoretical contribution. You will significantly amend or develop a new theory in your PhD if you want the doctorate to be awarded for a theoretical contribution. I also attempted to create a theoretical contribution in my PhD – a framework which I called the anti-dam protest cycle. I am not particularly proud of this attempt, though, and I have not even attempted publishing this in a peer-reviewed journal.

An empirical, methodological and/or theoretical contribution is needed for awarding a PhD. At least one of these types of contribution is also needed for publication in a peer-reviewed journal, whereas there are also an increasing number of cynics in the academy who claim that you can publish in peer-reviewed journals without making any contribution – and that this may even advance your career. 'Academia. Where it's better to have publications without insights than to have insight without publication' the saying goes. For those who are less cynical, any publication of PhD material in a journal signals that you have created a contribution with your work and this will facilitate your viva.

I attempted to signal that my work had created several contributions through the number of papers I published from my PhD data. The School of Geography and the Environment at the University of Oxford requires PhD students to have written four academic papers if the paper route is chosen. None of these papers need to be published upon submission of the PhD. However, they need to be 'worthy of publication',[190] according to the views of the PhD supervisors and assessors. Most PhD students at Oxford University will have published one paper upon submission of their thesis. I had published six papers out of my PhD research when I submitted my thesis. Sadly, several of these did not even count towards my PhD – including the one for which my undergraduate student colleague, Tim, had developed a financial model, as outlined in Chapter 3. However, many of these papers were published in some of the most prestigious journals in my field such as *Global Environmental Change* or *Journal of International Development*. Rushed research would not have made it into these journals, as both of my assessors knew.

If you have published a lot, your supervisor may also be more willing to let you graduate. You are a human resource from the perspective of your supervisor and letting you graduate usually means losing this human resource (or having to pay it (more) if you decide to stay with your supervisor as a postdoc upon graduation). There can thus be little incentive for your supervisor to accelerate your graduation. If you went above and beyond with your paper publications, though, most supervisors will be fair enough to let you go. Having published several papers evidences that you have done your work as a PhD student. And many supervisors may likely even ignore the quality of the 'coat' of your paper PhD if you have delivered several papers that they could co-author with you.

If I could do my PhD all over again, I would pay more attention to polishing my writing prior to submitting. This does not relate to my general writing, but rather typos and minor grammar mistakes. I would also pay more attention to my reference list. My assessors wrote regarding my initial submission that 'there are several stylistic problems – plenty of typographical errors particularly in the opening chapters' and that the 'bibliography also needs to be revised where references lack full Harvard referencing'. These types of issues evoke the impression that a PhD was rushed, whereas fixing these is straightforward. I used a professional copy-editing service to double-check my thesis prior to submitting my revisions. My girlfriend also helped. I now recommend to my PhD students to always use a professional copy-editing service (and/or their partner if they have a talent for copy-editing) for the initial submission of the PhD thesis. Some excellent copy-editing services provide their services for as little as GBP 0.01 per word.

▶ 4.5 Boosting the practical impact of the PhD

In theory, any start-up is about creating practical impact – which means sourcing customers and sales to these customers in the world of entrepreneurship. If no customer is interested in the start-up's offering, the start-up fails. In practice, many start-ups were theory-driven endeavours prior to the lean start-up movement. Founders would spend months writing elaborate business plans and honing their financial and marketing models instead of going out in the real world to test their core idea. Only the lean start-up movement ensured that founders focused on practical impact from Day 1, as outlined in Chapter 1 of this book.

Academics deal with two types of impact, as outlined previously: academic impact and practical impact. This book has been more concerned with academic impact so far. Sadly, academic impact, measured in citations, does not automatically translate into practical impact. For instance, the most cited article in the social sciences (excluding methodology articles) is 'The moderator-mediator variable distinction in social psychological research: conceptual, strategic, and statistical considerations', a 1986 piece written by Reuben Baron and David Kenny.[175,191] None of the practising psychologists I spoke to while writing this book had ever heard about this article and none of them could distinguish between moderator and mediator variables ad hoc. Admittedly, some highly cited works in the social sciences have had significant practical impact. For instance, the most cited social science book published before 1950 is *Das Kapital* by Karl Marx.[175]

Neither academic nor practical impact is required to pass a PhD. Indeed, most PhDs that are awarded (including the one by Jeffrey Sachs) do not contain a single line that has been cited even once at the time of submission. Furthermore, most practitioners are entirely unaware of most completed PhD dissertations that are directly related to their work. While impact is not necessary to pass a PhD, I encourage every PhD student to particularly think about how to accomplish practical impact. Even a student adhering to the lean PhD approach will spend a significant effort on their research. It would be a complete waste of time if none of this effort ever reached beyond the world of academia. The essence of knowledge is, having it, to apply it.[192]

The practical impact of research can be remarkable. Social science research shapes policies around the world. Meanwhile, natural science research has yielded inventions such as the pacemaker, safety glass, artificial sweetener and plastic.[193] Both types of research have created countless jobs – directly and indirectly. An example of direct job creation via both social and natural science research is the Cambridge Science Park, Europe's longest-serving and largest sciences park, located just outside Cambridge. It numbers 1,400 companies which employ more than 40,000 people.[192] Such start-ups are of great interest to policymakers since newly founded firms account for nearly all new job creation around the world.[192]

Accomplishing practical impact is challenging since the academy is geared much more towards academic impact. Professors are promoted if they publish as many

---

Try this … for boosting the practical implications of your PhD

- Write a newspaper commentary from your research results
- Ask your university press officer to publish a press release on your latest peer-reviewed paper
- Send your published work to those (including research subjects) that have contributed to it

---

peer-reviewed articles as possible in journals and thus also push their PhD students to focus on journal articles. Time spent on practical impact is time that could have also been spent on further improving that one journal article, many professors think. Those who aim for practical impact thus usually have a tough life.[192] However, there are several routes to practical impact which are not time-consuming and which can even feed into one's academic work again.

One of my preferred routes to ensure the practical impact of my research is to pen newspaper commentary. For instance, I wrote a piece in *Myanmar Times,* the oldest English-language newspaper in Myanmar, on why I think a particular dam project in Myanmar needs to be scrapped.[194] This piece was based on an peer-reviewed paper of mine that had unearthed some new information on this project.[90] The piece was shared more than 500 times on Facebook. As a follow-up, a journalist from the *New York Times* even reached out to me to enquire more about the project.

I also usually push the press officer at my current university to write a press release on any study I publish. This can also lead to a wider dissemination of one's work and thus practical impact. For instance, a press release by the University of Oxford regarding another paper of mine[120] also led to an enquiry by a journalist who then wrote an entire feature about my article. The journalist cited me in this feature several times.[195] The piece was shared more than 2,000 times on Facebook. It was thus probably read much more widely than the original academic paper which has only been downloaded around 200 times so far. Its key message was that activists are much more powerful in Myanmar than commonly perceived, a point that emerged from my research and which I wanted to bring across.

I also maintain an email list of everyone I interviewed for my research as well as relevant scholarly colleagues. Once typesetting for an accepted paper is completed (which means that the paper has been put into the layout of the journal; the paper will be published online one to two weeks after typesetting for most journals), I send it out to this list. Interviewees in particular are usually highly appreciative of this and frequently write back to me to share thoughts regarding my study – including critical ones – with me. This helps to sharpen my thinking which is reflected in my future writing on the topic (thus boosting academic quality and potential impact).

Many PhD students find their PhD to be all-encompassing, while their supervisors only push for academic quality and impact, as discussed previously. They thus do not feel they can spend time on any of the reach-outs I described above. I always challenge these students to reconsider. While writing a newspaper commentary does require some time (and there is no guarantee that a newspaper will publish it), convincing your press department to write a press release for you or sending out your paper to your interviewees and colleagues are activities that require minimum effort, maybe 30 minutes in total. Even the most all-encompassing PhD programme will be able to accommodate these 30 minutes. There is no excuse for not attempting to boost the practical impact of your PhD.

I undertook the reach-out activities described above throughout my PhD. If I could do my PhD again, I would intertwine academia and practice even more. I am currently involved in a research funding proposal that outlines a living lab approach for studying social entrepreneurship. A living lab approach is a user-centred research concept. The scholar immerses herself or himself in an environment and attempts to create solutions to problems encountered in this environment together with those regularly operating in this environment. The researcher is a researcher *and* study participant at the same time. Similarly, the study participant is a study participant *and* researcher at the same time. Solutions are co-created, immediately tested and refined based on end-user feedback, with the researchers recording the responses of the environment to the solutions tried out to enhance learning.[196] This type of research is the most applied research possible and I really think it may be the future of scholarship. I encourage my PhD students to embrace it for their work and I have one Master's student already embracing it. I share more about this in Chapter 5.

▶ 4.6 Quitting the PhD

One of the most popular mantras in the start-up community is 'quitters never win, winners never quit'.[197] It is also a mantra popular among those adhering to the lean start-up approach. Indeed, avoiding quitting is very much behind the lean start-up principles. Those who embrace them frequently argue that the lean start-up approach is all about 'failing fast'.[198] You build an MVP because you can

Insights from a PhD researcher

I am pursuing a part-time PhD which is not without its challenges, mainly because the real world – job, family and the need to have a life occasionally – all intervene. There is always a good reason for your research to get kicked into the long grass, but obviously that gets you nowhere. Although the time I can allocate to my PhD is limited, there are still ways to boost the practical impact of my research work. My research interests are broad: the business of media (business and revenue models), journalism innovation and changes in audience behaviours. These interests often coalesce, and I am seeking to bring these elements together on my research into the future of local news and, in particular, the future of local online journalism and local newspapers. I write frequently on these topics for a variety of traditional news outlets, an approach which I believe brings a variety of benefits to my PhD research. First, it helps me to sharpen my thinking because traditional news outlets typically require you to compress your story into 800 to 1,000 words. Second, it forces me to keep abreast of the latest developments, which is essential as I do not want my PhD to be rooted in the past. Finally, it also energizes me – in terms of seeing the impact of my research on readers (a mixture of industry and academic folk) and identifying potential research gaps (in terms of my own knowledge and the wider field), and it is also a fantastic way to find new case studies and potential interview subjects, due to the engagement I receive – post publication – from readers via email or social media. These facets all help to keep me on course, provide vital motivation and inspiration, and encourage me to keep going. I would really recommend to any PhD student to put yourself 'out there'. Of course, it takes time, but I believe that weaving this into your PhD approach can lead to richer, and more valuable, impactful, research. And that is a goal that, in my opinion, everyone can – and should – aspire to!

Damian Radcliffe, PhD Student (Journalism), Cardiff University, United Kingdom

then collect feedback from your end user as quickly as possible. If the end user does not embrace your idea after several rounds of rapid prototyping, you fail this idea, but you do not quit. The lean start-up approach attempts to create as much time as possible for failing to avoid quitting.

It has been claimed many times that most founders of a start-up fail. Popular media articles frequently outline that 90 per cent of start-ups fail.[199,200] The reality is not as grim, as already indicated in Chapter 1, although it is true that most start-ups fail. Cambridge Associates, a global investment firm based in Boston, the United States, tracked the performance of venture investments in 27,259 start-ups between 1990 and 2010. It found that the percentage of venture-backed start-ups that fail – as defined by companies that provide a basic return or less to investors – has not risen above 60 per cent since 2001.[38] This failure rate is comparable to that of PhD students, as already indicated in Chapter 1. Approximately 50 per cent of PhD students in the United States quit, according to one study.[39] Another study, the PhD Completion Project, which tracked 9,000 doctoral students in the United States and Canada from 30 different institutions from the early 1990s to 2004, found that 43 per cent who started their doctorates in the 1990s did not complete it within 10 years.[201] Of those PhD students that do quit, most do so in the first two years of their programme.[201]

'Should I quit my PhD or should I continue with it?' is a question that most PhD students have asked themselves at least once during their doctorate.[202] After all, any PhDs – including lean ones – will face crises since creating novel knowledge always entails encountering novel problems with no solutions yet created to overcome them. Crises are at the very heart of the research process – and not every crisis can be overcome. Anyone who has stayed in academia for a few years will be able to share many stories of projects that never led anywhere. Some professors now even publish their 'CV of failures' alongside their regular CVs.[203,204] Deciding if you will be able to overcome a crisis or not is difficult.[6] And you will lean more towards attempting to overcome a crisis if you have already invested a considerable amount of time and effort into your PhD programme – you will feel that this investment is wasted if you quit your research now.

I list some questions in Table 4.1 that you may ask yourself when considering quitting a PhD. These are based on a checklist used by some start-up founders who wanted to decide whether to proceed with their endeavour or not.

Table 4.1 'Quitting the PhD' checklist

#	Question	Answer
1	If I look back at the past six months: was I (mostly) miserable on a daily basis?	
2	Am I not passionate about my PhD topic (any more)?	
3	Is there something I feel passionate about pursuing professionally that is not my PhD?	
4	Is an academic career not appealing to me (any longer)?	
5	Have I not made substantial progress in my research in the past six months (according to my own standards of what constitutes 'progress')?	
6	If I have been in my PhD programme for at least two years: have I only received rejections from journals I have submitted to so far?	
7	Have I tried out at least two topics for my PhD which did not work out?	
8	Am I not getting along with my supervisor(s), no matter what?	

If you answer most of these questions with 'Yes', there are plenty of reasons to quit your PhD. However, even if you answered all questions with a 'Yes', you should not quit the PhD on the spur of the moment. Rushed decisions are rarely wise ones. I suggest talking to your supervisors and mentors about your plans to quit. Also talk to your family, partner and friends. Deliberate on why you enrolled in the PhD in the first place and if you think there is anything that you may be able to do to reinvigorate your original reasons to pursue a PhD. Then wait. Wait a week and ask yourself if you still want to quit the PhD. If the answer is still 'Yes', wait another week. If the answer is still 'Yes' after a month, it may be time to quit your PhD.

Scientists have created the world we live in and this impact is one reason why so many people want to pursue a PhD. We could not wash our dishes in the evening or turn on the computer in the morning without scientists. There would be no cars, trains or planes without scientists.[205] In the early twentieth century, the worldwide average life expectancy did not exceed 40 years. Today, the average stands at around 70.[206] The single cause for this miraculous leap is the ability of medics to cure diseases – an ability which grew exponentially in the past century. Vaccines, antibiotics and further advances in medical technology have fundamentally changed the game.

Another reason drawing students to the academy may be the stardom which is granted to those at the very top of their fields. A star academic I particularly admire is Jeffrey Sachs. The Columbia University economist has authored three *New York Times* bestsellers and has been named twice among the 100 most influential world leaders by *Time* magazine.[192] He is Special Advisor to United Nations Secretary-General António Guterres on Sustainable Development Goals, and previously advised UN Secretary-General Ban Ki-moon on both the Sustainable Development Goals and Millennium Development Goals. In the 1980s he helped several Latin American countries including Bolivia, Brazil and Peru to end hyperinflation and to renegotiate their external debts.[174]

Many of us social scientists want to be Jeffrey Sachs. However, there is tremendous potential for impact beyond the academy as well. And sometimes those who quit their PhD go on to change the world most. We are bombarded by stories praising the value of persistence, while we do not hear enough about the benefits of quitting. But there are times when we need to acknowledge that we have hung on to a dream, e.g. completing a PhD, for too long. The most famous example of an extremely successful PhD drop-out may be Elon Musk, the CEO of SpaceX, Tesla and one of the co-founders of PayPal. Musk enrolled in a PhD programme in applied physics at Stanford University. He dropped out 48 hours later to develop Zip2, a company that created online city guides for newspaper publishers. Four years later, he sold this business for USD 340 million.[207] 'When

I was in college, I wanted to be involved in things that would change the world', he reportedly said.[208] Evidently, he did not feel that a PhD in applied physics would help him do so. His vita evidences that not finishing a dissertation is not a disaster. Instead, it can be a blessing.

There are countless examples of graduate students who quit their PhDs and find fulfilment and impact in careers beyond academia. A less well-known example than Elon Musk is Kate Zmich who enrolled in a PhD in education at the University of Delaware in the autumn of 2010. She dropped out the following spring and now works as an operations manager for the Smith Memorial Playground in Philadelphia, a non-profit organization that provides opportunities for unstructured creative play for children 10 years of age and younger. Vanessa Vaile, who started a PhD in comparative literature in 1992 at the University of California, Davis, remained in the programme for seven years. During this time, she completed all but her dissertation before she decided to drop out. She now runs Mountainair Online, a community website featuring local news and announcements.[201]

If you only pursue a PhD for 48 hours, as Elon Musk did, few skills will be gained. However, if you enrol in a PhD for a year or longer, and then decide to drop out, you may have gained various skills that are transferable to and valuable in many jobs outside the academy. Even after a few months in a PhD programme, you will have gained specialist cutting-edge knowledge in a specific area that many employers may find interesting. Furthermore, any PhD student (including the one dropping out) is trained to pay attention to detail – a skill relevant in many professions. And every PhD student will have encountered enormous challenges. While they may not have overcome them all by the time they drop out, they will certainly have learnt much from this failure that may be useful in their next endeavour.

The lean PhD even offers skills on top of the traditional PhD approach. You will be used to working based on deadlines and creating good-enough products. The lean PhD will also make you an expert in dealing with feedback. Furthermore, it teaches you how to successfully create and manage teams. Most importantly, you are prepared to join any organization that embraces lean methodologies if you have worked with the lean PhD approach throughout your doctorate. I shared in the preface of this book that firms such as AT&T, the world's largest telecommunications company,[18] Nokia Siemens Networks, a major data networking player, and *The Washington Post*, a prestigious newspaper, have all adopted lean principles.[19] Even governments in the most remote parts of the world nowadays work with these principles. Your way of working will immediately click with these organizations if you embraced the lean PhD approach throughout your doctorate.

A skill not gained as much if embracing the lean PhD approach compared to the traditional one may be working independently. Those who embrace the lean PhD do not follow the paradigm of the 'lone scholar', as discussed in Chapter 3. This may be welcomed by most firms, though, since most jobs require teamwork. Indeed, if you embraced the lean approach throughout their PhD may want to highlight in any application materials that you are a team player.

You may still receive many rejections. Sabine Kobayter from the *Huffington Post* recently wrote in a commentary on PhD students that 'the real world doesn't necessarily welcome them with open arms'.[209] Indeed, one-third of doctorate recipients report no firm employment upon graduation[210] and 40 per cent of those with a doctorate eventually end up in non-research roles[6] (one reason may be that 80 per cent of postdocs earn less than the average construction worker[211]). Hence, considering the skills that you have gained throughout your doctorate (no matter if you have completed it or not) and their relevance for the labour market beyond academia is essential. If you eventually shift to a position that is not a research-intense one, this shift can be smoother if you thoroughly understand your skillset.

A sector particularly suited to those who consider exiting the academy during or after their (lean) PhD may be management consulting. Many management consultancies work lean, as discussed previously, and need team players. They need staff that can create good-enough products within a tight timeframe. They need staff that can solve tough problems and that have attention to detail. And your specialist knowledge may even be of immense value for some boutique consultancies out there. Another advantage of management consulting is that you can advance relatively fast if you are willing to put in the hours, and some may want this after having spent years in junior positions in academia while their friends from high school have already advanced to senior levels in the corporate world. Whenever I think about quitting the academy, the one sector I therefore think about first is management consulting.

5 Towards Lean Science

This chapter explains:

- The lean PhD approach in a nutshell
- The case for the lean PhD in a nutshell
- How to make the transition to lean science

▶ 5.1 The lean PhD (in a nutshell)

The lean PhD approach is an attempt to re-envision the PhD as we currently pursue it.[212] The PhD student in the lean PhD is a start-up. Just as with the start-up, the student starts as a one-person show. Both the PhD student and the start-up founder are tasked with creating something novel from scratch. Both must accomplish this task with only limited resources. The novelty of these endeavours implies permanent uncertainties regarding the road ahead – with the only certainty being that it will most likely prove thorny. Launching, executing and exiting a successful start-up is incredibly difficult – 60 per cent of start-up founders fail.[38] Launching, executing and exiting a successful PhD start-up is also incredibly difficult – up to 50 per cent of PhD students who enrol into a PhD never complete it.[39]

Start-ups have been able to significantly boost their chances of succeeding in recent years via the lean start-up approach. Start-ups such as Dropbox, Spotify and Instagram have used it. As we saw in Chapter 1, Dropbox managed to reach one million users after only seven months,[46] Spotify after five months.[47] Meanwhile, it took Instagram only 2.5 months to gain its first one million users.[48] While completing a PhD in only 2.5 months (or five months or seven months) may be out of reach (at least for now), PhD students can learn much from the working approaches these start-ups have adopted. Indeed, emulating them can result in a radically more successful PhD.

Some start-ups are stuck in excessive whiteboarding, which is a symptom of bureaucratic overthinking and which only results in an analysis paralysis. These are the start-ups that go bust. Lean start-ups do not excessively whiteboard. These start-ups build a minimum viable product (MVP) which is a product that entails the core features of their envisaged final product as quickly as possible with the fewest resources possible. This product is then improved via rapid prototyping with the start-up collecting feedback from the envisaged end user again and again to introduce targeted improvements. These 'build-measure-learn' loops are virtuous cycles that vastly accelerate the start-up's journey towards success.

Because the PhD is such a complex endeavour, it can seem overwhelming – particularly in the very beginning. The lean PhD canvas – an adaptation of the lean canvas that start-up founders use to structure the early days of their endeavour – helps the PhD student to tackle the early days of their own start-up. The lean PhD canvas outlines the core questions to ask and the core decisions to undertake when you are about to start your PhD. One of the most critical questions to decide upon is which academic market to target. The lean PhD student avoids the crowded markets, but rather focuses on the niche markets that are on an upward trajectory. These are the markets where incumbents are unlikely to outwit the lean PhD student – and thus just the right markets for the lean PhD student to disrupt the academy.

The MVP in the launch phase of the PhD is the lean research proposal. Rapid prototyping for this MVP is undertaken (mostly) via the envisaged PhD supervisor. The lean PhD student does not reach out to the envisaged supervisor via an elaborate research proposal. Rather, the lean PhD student reaches out with a set of possible research ideas that could be at the centre of the research proposal. Suitable questions are chosen jointly with the supervisor and further developed with their feedback. Friends and family may provide additional feedback. The early career supervisor is to be preferred over the star professor because this supervisor is hungry for success and thus more likely to invest the feedback time needed for the lean PhD to succeed. The lean PhD student agreed with her or his supervisor early on in the PhD process that a paper-based PhD will be written since papers are much more compact and thus suitable for iteration than a traditional thesis. The supervisor whose research interests are reflected in the PhD student's research proposal is also an important ally for the PhD student to identify funding sources for his work.

Once the PhD student is admitted, they start creating the first minimum viable paper of their PhD. Paper publications ensure an accelerated PhD defence. The end user for any paper written throughout the lean PhD is the anonymous peer reviewer of an academic journal. To create a minimum viable paper, the lean PhD student must start writing as soon as possible. Lean start-ups work via learning-by-doing. Lean PhD students work via learning-by-writing. The lean PhD student is not ashamed of bullet point drafts and half-baked manuscripts.

Rather, the lean PhD student embraces these to be able to collect thorough feedback as soon as possible.

The lean PhD student knows that more feedback strengthens the impact of build-measure-learn loops. Feedback is a gift. The first provider of feedback is the lean PhD student's supervisor(s). More feedback is provided on the minimum viable paper by scholars beyond the supervisor(s). These selected scholars are chosen because of their specific theoretical and methodological knowledge on a paper project. Practitioners may also be added to a paper project because they may be able to provide access to difficult-to-reach populations. The lean PhD student is pragmatic, adding star academics as co-authors to their paper project (even if they turn out to add very little) since their name on the paper increases the chances of publishing in a renowned journal. Furthermore, the lean PhD student sees undergraduate and graduate students as an integral part of their team for a paper project. These students can help with data collection, undertake literature reviews – and often also complete more challenging tasks. Students supporting a paper project are also the co-authors of this project and the lean PhD student is their mentor.

The lean PhD student who executes the PhD is also a conference junkie. They see conferences as sounding boards for their ideas. The lean PhD student goes to conferences particularly when they are stuck, knowing that the audience will help to unstuck them. However, there may also be times where an idea does not fly – despite major efforts undertaken. The lean PhD student is not one that is glued to their idea. Rather, the lean PhD student is ready to kill their darling. If there is repeatedly no encouraging feedback from the academic community regarding a selected paper project and thus no progress in making a contribution, the lean PhD student says 'Next!'. Pivoting is at the core of executing the lean PhD.

The lean PhD is ultimately about exiting. The lean PhD student does not want to exit with the most polished dissertation imaginable. Rather, they aim for a minimum viable dissertation (MVD). The assessors of this dissertation are the lean PhD student's allies in further honing it. The lean PhD student chooses these (via their supervisor) strategically – just as the start-up founder will not sell out to any company. The ideal assessor is the one whose work the PhD student has advanced via their dissertation. The lean PhD student is keen for the assessors' feedback and thus keen to undertake revisions after the defence. The assessors will not think that the MVD is a cheap dissertation because the lean PhD student has gone the extra mile. They may have collected the largest dataset ever on the chosen topic or they will have at least one or two publications in renowned peer-reviewed journals which signal the outstanding quality of the work undertaken.

The lean PhD student has also already undertaken numerous efforts to boost the practical implications of their work, not only after but during the PhD.

The lean PhD student writes newspaper articles about their work. They also persuade the university's press officer to pen a release on any paper published out of the PhD. The lean PhD student follows up with their research subjects, sharing the work that is based on interactions with these subjects. The lean PhD student is not distant from their research subjects. Rather, they want to jointly work with them to bring about impact and change.

The chances to succeed as a PhD student may be vastly increased by adopting the approach outlined in this book. Yet there is no guarantee that you will succeed if you adopt this approach. And it is okay for the lean PhD student to quit. This is not a decision they will undertake overnight. Rather, it is one that will be conscious and thus one that the lean PhD student will not regret at a later stage. There is much impact that the academy can exert on society. This is the reason why the lean PhD student has launched their start-up in the first place. Yet there is also much impact you can have outside of academia. Indeed, change is not restricted to a specific sector.

The most important stakeholder for the lean PhD student is their supervisor. You need your supervisor to be invested in your endeavour. The supervisor does not necessarily need to be invested in the lean PhD approach, though. I never shared this approach with my supervisors because I do not believe much in theorizing but in results speaking for themselves. Because of the results I produced my supervisors were always invested in my work – and provided the feedback that I needed to succeed in my research. If your supervisor only wants to see you every other month, if they need half a year to provide feedback on your draft, if they do not want you to succeed, you will not succeed. You must find another supervisor then or, if this is not possible, quit your PhD.

Great supervisors can be found in every discipline. Hence, the lean PhD approach is applicable to every discipline. The biologist will benefit from going for a lean research proposal just as much as the philosopher. The engineer will benefit from starting to write as early as possible just as much as the anthropologist. And it makes sense to go for an MVD instead of a seemingly perfect one for the physicist, the medic and the geographer. You *can* go for the lean PhD approach if you want to. There are no excuses. The lean PhD approach can be a game changer for your PhD.

▶ 5.2 The case for the lean PhD

This book is about the lean PhD. Tens of thousands of PhD theses are typed up each year.[100] Not all who pursue a PhD will likely read this book. My publisher asked me to calculate how many PhD students (and PhD supervisors and other people interested in this) will buy this book when I first proposed this endeavour. I estimated that 100,000 people may buy it – admittedly, a very aggressive estimate, considering that *The Lean Startup* by Eric Ries only sold around 100,000 copies, as outlined earlier[54,55] (I assume that there are more start-up founders around the world that speak English than PhD students, but there seem to be no solid statistics available to back these assumptions).

Let us assume that I was wrong with my estimate by a factor of 10. Hence, 10,000 copies of this book would sell. If we assume that the average PhD takes 48 months and every person who reads it manages to reduce their PhD completion time by 27 months (again, this is a somewhat aggressive estimate, but we just went conservative with the projected commercial success of this book), this means that this book may save its readers a total of 270,000 months, or 22,500 years. Again, even if I am wrong with this estimate again by a factor of 10 (and this book then saves 2,250 years), this will have been the most impactful work I have created so far. And I would be so excited about this for you.

After all, the PhD (mostly) does not make much sense if you purely look at it from an income perspective. Yet this income perspective is important to many who pursue it for careers outside of the academy (which is entirely legitimate and often even a wise choice). The traditional PhD may take you four years or even longer and it only commands an income premium over a Master's degree (which you can complete in less than a year) of 3 per cent, according to one estimate.[211] And even this meagre premium may be exaggerated for many PhD students, given that this statistic also includes the business administration PhD student who starts a highly paid middle management position immediately after their PhD or the law PhD who starts an (even more) highly paid job at a law firm immediately after their PhD. If you complete the PhD faster, even by just two or three months, you will increase your PhD premium. Any day you can save on your PhD can be one where you will earn more in another job.

People who are passionate about research are the ones who do one postdoc after the other, continuing to hope for that tenure-track position. Some more data on them: I already outlined that 80 per cent of postdocs earn less than the average construction worker.[211] However, the postdoc earns more than the PhD student, at least. One study, published in *Nature Biotechnology,* looked at what happens after the postdoc if you do not make it into an academic position. The study found that, on average, you give up about one-fifth of your earning potential in the first 15 years after finishing your doctorate if you first do a postdoc but then switch to an industry position (compared to someone who immediately switches to an industry position).[213] 'That's evidence that a postdoc has little value outside of academia', the lead author of that study says.[214] If you start in industry instead of pursuing a postdoc you can usually expect a salary that is twice as high as that of a postdoc. The only exception to this are those who pursue PhDs in the humanities and arts; then your salary will be about as meagre (USD 50,000 per year) as a postdoc as it would be in industry.[215] (If you care a lot about income, though, data also suggests that you should spend little time studying for degrees at all: the average college grade point average (GPA) of American millionaires is 2.9 – not enough to make it into even a mediocre PhD programme;[216] the average college GPA for Americans is 3.1.[217])

Sadly, data on long-term career outcomes on PhD students is scarce. One study from the late 1990s found that 53 per cent of those who pursue a PhD want to become professors. However, only half of that group had obtained a permanent academic position within 10 to 14 years after their PhD, while 33 per cent who wanted to become professors had left the academy by then. The regional focus of this study was the United States.[218,219] More recent data indicates that the odds of landing a professorship have further worsened in recent years. One study from the United Kingdom outlines that of every 200 people who complete a PhD, only seven will get a permanent academic post and only one will become a professor. We are suffering a glut of PhDs who cannot find academic jobs.[220]

People invest much to stay in the academy – and many may invest too much. Forty per cent of instructors in colleges in the United States are now adjuncts.[221] These are part-time, precarious jobs with no health insurance or the kind of other benefits usually associated with a standard employment relationship. Many adjuncts make less money than campus support staff who may not even have a college degree.[222] One adjunct professor with a PhD in medieval history reported to take home no more than GBP 680 per month. She has to rely on food stamps.[222] Another adjunct professor was recently reported in *The Guardian* to have turned to sex work to complement her meagre academic income.[223] This news is shocking even for those who do not care much about income prospects (which is the case for most in the academy).

These extreme examples may best illustrate why some have compared contemporary academia to a pyramid scheme.[224,225] A pyramid scheme is a business model that lures in new members with the promise of a lucrative pay-out. However, the players at the top profit by far the most, at the expense of those at the bottom.[226] I find this to be an accurate metaphor. PhD students and other early career researchers (including adjunct professors) are paid much less than those Master's students that seek a gig outside of the academy, although the former have often been at the very top of their class.[227] While most PhD students are aware that landing a professorship is difficult, few supervisors share with them just how difficult it will be. And even fewer professors will share with those they hire as postdocs or adjuncts the odds regarding their future careers, while they benefit (as a co-author) from each publication the postdoc churns out or from the reduced teaching load that adjuncts create for the full professors who then have more time for their research.

This may read as disillusioning. And it is meant to be disillusioning. After all, one effective option to increase the odds regarding an academic career for those that pursue a PhD is to radically reduce the number of PhD students.[228] There are more and more PhD students enrolling every year in many countries around the world, while fewer and fewer permanent academic positions are available.[225] I am changing the metaphor that I have employed throughout this book a bit now: imagine a start-up where 50 per cent of employees at the entry level quit. There must be some mad boss at this start-up. You would not want to work at it. Yet up to 50 per cent of PhD students fail and more and more still enrol. The academic job market is brutal, and there is an urgent need for anyone who wants to enter this system to face these realities to be able to appropriately react to them.

Because the academic job market is brutal, you must excel in your PhD if you want to stand a chance. If you are up for this pyramid scheme, you want to reach the top of this scheme as fast as possible. If you do not excel, this book has helped you to cut your losses since I hope you will be able to complete your PhD more efficiently by reading this book. However, the lean PhD is not merely an efficient PhD. It is also meant as a guide to a PhD that is of higher quality and greater impact than one you would have produced with the traditional approach.

Sadly, higher quality and greater impact is no guarantee for an academic job. While the academy frequently prides itself on being a meritocracy,[229] it is not. Just 18 elite universities produce half of all computer science professors, 16 schools produce half of all business professors and eight schools account for half of all history professors in the United States, although there are many extremely productive PhD students (with productivity measured by the number of publications in prestigious peer-reviewed journals) at many other universities as well, as outlined earlier in this book.[85,86] Comparable studies have been carried out for many other countries around the world.[230-233] For instance, one study found that even in Sweden, a country famous for its meritocratic values, 30 per cent of academic employees are on short-term contracts that were never advertised which means that these are jobs that were provided via networks. At the same time, 60 per cent of Swedish academics work at their doctoral alma maters. This is academic inbreeding instead of hiring the best and brightest.[232]

While networks are crucial for academic advancement (and possibly more crucial for this advancement than high-quality work with impact), I very much believe we still need to relentlessly focus on the quality and impact of our work as academics. If we abandon this focus, we can abandon the entire academic enterprise. An academy without this relentless focus on quality and impact best remains in its ivory tower because it will do more harm than good outside of it. We must focus on quality and impact just for the sake of quality and impact or there is nothing left that is worthwhile in the academy. Meanwhile, the excellent academic paper that stirred much discussion inside and outside of the academy will always open many more doors for you (inside and outside of the academy) than the dull one that nobody took any notice of. There is no malus for quality and impact.

Quality and impact of academic work is generated in the lean PhD by rapid iteration. You iterate with your supervisor. You iterate with additional co-authors. You iterate via conferences. You iterate with anonymous peer reviewers. You iterate with your assessors. Iteration creates quality and an audience for your work which is the precondition for academic as well as societal impact. Iteration with this variety of stakeholders helps to ensure you develop an end product that is considered to be of quality by the relevant stakeholders.

Because the lean PhD approach is about efficiency and quality and impact, it is not an approach that needs to be masked if you adopt it. I believe in results instead of talking. Hence I never explained my working approach to my PhD supervisors in detail, as outlined earlier, while my supervisors were intrigued by my way of working. 'When I saw how and how fast Julian could create quality work, I knew he would be able to complete his PhD in less than two years', one of my supervisors said after my viva. You may explain your (lean) working approach to your supervisors if you think it may improve your working relationships with them. Any suitable supervisor will be supportive of a working approach that creates higher quality and impact than a traditional working approach, and in less time.

▶ 5.3 Towards lean science

Many academics I talk to say that the academy must change – and that it will change because everybody says that it must change. While there are many analyses out there on the many problems the contemporary academy is facing, there are far fewer proposed solutions. This book is meant as a solution. It has proposed the lean PhD approach, an approach fundamentally at odds with how many PhDs are pursued these days. This lean PhD approach is grounded in the story of my PhD. I shared with you how I approached launching, executing and exiting my PhD. I hope that this has generated some ideas for you on how you go about your own PhD. I have now become an academic and my impression is that many of the working principles I outlined in this book may not only be applicable to the PhD, but to the entire academy. This section outlines how.

I argued in Chapter 2 of this book for a lean research proposal. Yet academics do not write research proposals when applying for their PhD position only. Rather, academics write research proposals all the time. Indeed, I have not done much else this month besides finishing this manuscript. Many of those who fund research require extremely elaborate proposals. Months on months are spent on developing these, while most of them are eventually rejected. For instance, 94 per cent of proposals for European Union (EU) funding are rejected.[234] Writing these proposals is thus an extremely unproductive activity for scholars. Most scholars should rather spend their time on something else.

When I talk to those who assess these proposals, I am told that many can be rejected from a perfunctory first sight. For instance, the topic may not fit the interests of the funder or the composition of the consortium may be an issue. A two-stage process could have saved both the applicant and the funder much time. This would mean that only a one-pager with the core idea and team is submitted for the first round and then only those proposals that the funder finds truly worthwhile will pass this round. This one-pager would be the lean research proposal in academia beyond the PhD. Admittedly, some funders, e.g. VW Foundation,[235] already have such a two-stage process in place (even those awarding EU funding are increasingly using it[234]), but many others do not.

I argued in Chapter 3 of this book for a minimum viable paper. Producing papers remains the core task throughout an academic's entire career and there is no reason why the principles outlined in Chapter 3 should not be applied while writing any academic paper. Indeed, I push for this approach at my current university, Utrecht University, every day, no matter if I write a paper with one of my PhD students or with another professor. The more feedback you collect prior to submission of a paper, the better this paper will be, and conceptualizing the anonymous reviewers as your allies in further honing your paper only helps you to get your manuscript out.[236]

Meanwhile, I argued in Chapter 4 in favour of the minimum viable dissertation (MVD). Most people only write one PhD dissertation (there are exceptions, though. For instance, one partner at the Berlin office of a well-known consulting firm has written two PhD dissertations; consequently, many people now address him as 'Dr Dr'). While you may only write one PhD dissertation in your life and may thus only face your PhD assessors once in your life, you will continue to be assessed by your employer even if you become a full professor (at least in most countries around the world). These assessments consider how much and where you have published, if your work is recognized by the relevant scientific community, how much funding you bring in and how your students evaluate you as a teacher. Many see those providing feedback to their work as antagonists.

The lean PhD approach rather suggests seeing them as (potential) allies that can help you shape your path in the academy.

I have claimed throughout this book that the lean PhD is about a PhD that is more efficient than the traditional one, while producing higher quality as well as more academic and societal impact. Yet the reader will have noticed that I have usually been more concerned with academic than societal impact. I suggested catering the lean research proposal to the supervisor, the minimum viable paper to the anonymous reviewers of journals and the MVD to the assessors – these target groups are all academic. And I stand by this advice. The PhD student who is keen to accelerate their PhD journey must first focus on stakeholders in academia since it is these who eventually award the PhD. There is no way to change this for the PhD student. At the same time, though, there are always also pathways for the PhD student to maximize their work's societal impact – and the PhD student should embrace these. Even a single press release may contribute to societal impact, as I outlined in Chapter 4.

Yet let us imagine an academy that does not focus on academic impact, but on societal impact. Sadly, there is often a discrepancy between the two, at least for the social sciences I attempt to contribute to. Here is a recent example from my own work: I now need to focus on academic impact as an early career scholar. When deciding what paper to write next, I thus specifically searched papers that are highly cited. I found a paper entitled 'How corporate social responsibility is defined: an analysis of 37 definitions' by Alexander Dahlsrud.[237] This piece has been cited more than 2,700 times. It is a wonderful paper from an academic perspective. Corporate social responsibility (CSR) is a fuzzy and contested term with many definitions, while any paper on CSR still needs to define it (you just define your core term in an academic paper). If you pick any definition of CSR, it seems arbitrary. Dahlsrud has solved this problem by aggregating the different definitions into a meta-definition. By adopting this definition, you can thus claim to adopt a seemingly objective definition and move on in your paper.

I have recently published 'Conceptualizing the circular economy: an analysis of 114 definitions', a piece inspired by Dahlsrud. It attempts to create a meta-definition for the term 'circular economy', which may be even more contested than CSR.[238,239] As expected, the paper became an academic hit. For instance, it is now in the top 5 per cent of all research outputs ever tracked by Altmetric[240] and currently the most downloaded article in the journal I published it in. Yet most practitioners could not care less about a meta-definition of CSR or the circular economy. Businesses, rather, want to know how to overcome barriers they encounter when attempting to adopt CSR programmes or circular economy approaches, while governments are keen to understand how to convince businesses to adopt these in the first place and how an adoption that has taken place can be accelerated.

If I was asked not to showcase how many citations my work is creating (and thus what academic impact I have), but what impact my work has on business practice or governments I would write entirely different papers. I am already attempting to devote at least some of my time to such papers. For instance, one of my Master's students is now working on the circular economy in the coffee industry. For this work, at the beginning of his thesis he gathered several players from a selected coffee industry supply chain for a workshop. These then jointly developed measures with him to increase the circularity in the supply chain, e.g. measures to boost recycling or reuse, and commit to implementing them in the next few months. For his Master's thesis, my student is observing how this implementation is working out, describing successes in detail as well as barriers that are encountered and how these are overcome at times. This kind of action research is not only extremely energizing for the student, but also most instructive for any business that wants to go circular.

I also much admire the research by the first supervisor of my PhD. She is the co-director of REACH, a research programme funded by the United Kingdom's Department for International Development (DFID),[241] that aims to improve water security for millions of poor people in Africa and South Asia by delivering world-class science that transforms policy and practice. The programme does not only generate new evidence on water security, but also establishes partnerships between science and practitioners to translate this evidence into action while also training the next generation of water managers in Africa and Asia in the latest approaches in water security.

Admittedly, this kind of work may be difficult to carry out in some disciplines. If you are pursuing work in history or English literature, there is evidently a lack of players who will be able to do action research with you. Yet a focus on societal impact in these disciplines may also reveal a different type of work. It may be work that is written in a way that is more accessible to the public and/or connected a lot more to the public discourse. At the same time, my impression is that many of the natural sciences already carry out much work that is focused on a societal end user instead of an academic one. There may be much social scientists can learn from natural scientists in this regard.

One of my professors from my Master's degree recently shared on Facebook that our responsibility [as academics] is to help build a better society. Academics have a bargain with society. We are given time and space and money to think, and in return we are supposed to give back creative ideas, to make life better for society.[242]

I could not agree more strongly with this. At the same time, I do not think that many of us in the academy are fulfilling our part of this bargain. Admittedly, there is a trend in some academic systems towards lean approaches and more societal impact. For instance, Steve Blank, an entrepreneur turned academic, is pushing business professors in the United States to orientate their work much more towards their societal end user, businesses.[243] But many more of these initiatives are needed. If societal impact becomes the core criterion for academic research, we may no longer investigate meta-definitions for a specific term. Some may complain about this. But there is so much more to gain than to lose when abandoning the obsession with academic impact to focus on the betterment of society. This is the most fundamental component and ultimate aim of lean science.

References

1. Haidar, H. What is a PhD? *QS* (2014). Available at: https://www.topuniversities. com/blog/what-phd. Accessed on 5 February 2018.
2. Becker, J. Zeitspanne der Promotion: Dauer im Durchschnitt. (2017). Available at: https://www.academics.de/ratgeber/promotion-dauer. Accessed on 5 February 2018.
3. Katyan, M. How do you compare a PhD in Europe vs. a PhD in USA? *www. admissiontable.com* (2017). Available at: https://www.admissiontable.com/ how-do-you-compare-pursuing-a-phd-in-europe-vs-a-phd-in-usa/. Accessed on 5 February 2018.
4. Berger, J. Exploring ways to shorten the ascent to a Ph.D. *New York Times* (2007). Available at: http://www.nytimes.com/2007/10/03/education/03education. html. Accessed on 5 February 2018.
5. Kousha, K. & Thelwall, M. *Are Wikipedia Citations Important Evidence of the Impact of Scholarly Articles and Books?* (Journal of the Association for Information Science and Technology, 2015).
6. Science. Quitting, or not Quitting a PhD. (2004). Available at: http://www. sciencemag.org/careers/2004/03/quitting-or-not-quitting-phd. Accessed on 5 February 2018.
7. Dunleavy, P. *Authoring a PhD: How to Plan, Draft, Write, and Finish a Doctoral Thesis or Dissertation.* (Palgrave Macmillan, 2003).
8. Billig, M. *Learn to Write Badly: How to Succeed in the Social Sciences.* (Cambridge University Press, 2013).
9. Glatthorn, A. & Joyner, R. *Writing the Winning Thesis or Dissertation. A Step-by-Step Guide.* (SAGE Publications, 2005).
10. White, B. *Mapping Your Thesis. The Comprehensive Manual of Theory and Techniques for Masters and Doctoral Research.* (ACER Press, 2011).
11. Thomson, P. & Walker, M. *The Routledge Doctoral Student Companion: Getting to Grips with Research in Education and the Social Sciences.* (Routledge, 2010).
12. Murray, R. *How to Write a Thesis.* (Open University Press, 2011).
13. Becker, H. S. *Tricks of the Trade: How to Think about Your Research While You're Doing It.* (University of Chicago Press, 1998).

14. QS. QS World University Rankings by Subject 2016 – Geography & Area Studies. (2016). Available at: https://www.topuniversities.com/university-rankings/ university-subject-rankings/2016/geography. Accessed on 5 February 2018.

15. Matthews, D. Universities whose work has driven environmental awareness. (2016). Available at: https://www.timeshighereducation.com/news/ universities-whose-work-has-driven-environmental-awareness. Accessed on 5 February 2018.

16. Ries, E. *The Lean Startup: How Constant Innovation Creates Radically Successful Businesses.* (Penguin Books, 2011).

17. Holweg, M. The genealogy of lean production. *J. Oper. Manag.* **25**, 420–437 (2007).

18. Forbes. World's 25 biggest telecom companies in 2017. (2017). Available at: https://www.forbes.com/pictures/591b6ecf31358e03e559255f/2017-global-2000-telecom/#66bdd5f045f2. Accessed on 5 February 2018.

19. Shaughnessy, H. The rise of lean and why it matters. *Forbes* (2013). Available at: https://www.forbes.com/sites/haydnshaughnessy/2013/01/04/the-rise-of-lean-and-why-it-matters/#c2c9677136f7. Accessed on 5 February 2018.

20. Shontell, A. This is the definitive definition of a startup. *Business Insider* (2014). Available at: http://www.businessinsider.com/what-is-a-startup-definition-2014-12?international=true&r=US&IR=T. Accessed on 5 February 2018.

21. Dhoul, T. Stanford GSB: class of 2015 employment report. (2015). Available at: https://www.topmba.com/jobs/career-trends/stanford-gsb-class-2015-employment-report. Accessed on 5 February 2018.

22. Hill, C. 5 once-prestigious jobs that are now B-list. *MarketWatch* (2015). Available at: http://www.marketwatch.com/story/5-once-prestigious-jobs-that-are-now-b-list-2015-01-13. Accessed on 5 February 2018.

23. Dunleavy, P. Assessing your research and publication choices. (2015). Available at: https://medium.com/advice-and-help-in-authoring-a-phd-or-non-fiction/ assessing-your-research-and-publication-choices-316a36d28263. Accessed on 5 February 2018.

24. Shontell, A. The most difficult hurdle to overcome in a startup's first year may be psychological. *Business Insider* (2013). Available at: http://www.business insider.com/loneliness-and-startups-2013-7?IR=T. Accessed on 5 February 2018.

25. Newman, K. M. Startup CEO: the loneliest job in the world? *tech.co* (2015). Available at: https://tech.co/startup-ceo-loneliest-job-in-the-world-2015-01. Accessed on 5 February 2018.

26. Pilbeam, C. & Denyer, D. Lone scholar or community member? The role of student networks in doctoral education in a UK management school. *Stud. High. Educ.* **34**, 301–318 (2009).

27. Levecque, K., Anseel, F., De Beuckelaer, A., Van der Heyden, J. & Gisle, L. Work organization and mental health problems in PhD students. *Res. Policy* **46**, 868–879 (2017).

28. www.africanprintinfashion.com. The Fashion Deli: 'We want to disrupt the market!' (2015). Available at: https://www.africanprintinfashion.com/2015/05/the-fashion-deli-we-want-to-disrupt-the-market.html. Accessed on 5 February 2018.

29. University of Cambridge. PhD, MSc, MLitt and MPhil by dissertation. (2017). Available at: http://www.cambridgestudents.cam.ac.uk/your-course/examinations/graduate-exam-information/writing-submitting-and-examination/phd-msc-mlitt. Accessed on 5 February 2018.

30. University of Warwick. Requirements for the award of research degrees. (2017). Available at: https://www2.warwick.ac.uk/study/postgraduate/research/phdbypublishedwork/guidance_on_requirements_for_the_award_of_research_degrees.pdf. Accessed on 5 February 2018.

31. Hoovers. Litmus Software, inc. Revenue and financial data. (2017). Available at: http://www.hoovers.com/company-information/cs/revenue-financial.litmus_software_inc.ec4db08fd7b66fb3.html. Accessed on 5 February 2018.

32. Patel, S. Growing a startup without funding: how 5 entrepreneurs made bootstrapping work. *Forbes* (2016). Available at: https://www.forbes.com/sites/sujanpatel/2016/10/08/growing-a-startup-without-funding/2/#64a30b2bffae. Accessed on 5 February 2018.

33. Frassdorf, A., Kaulisch, M. & Hornbostel, S. Armut und Ausbeutung? *academics.de* (2012). Available at: https://www.academics.de/wissenschaft/armut_und_ausbeutung_52988.html.

34. Chiose, S. A PhD does pay off – at 40. *The Globe and Mail* (2013). Available at: https://www.theglobeandmail.com/news/national/education/a-phd-does-pay-off-at-40/article11713827/. Accessed on 5 February 2018.

35. Tape, C. J. Creative crash. (2015). Available at: http://christape.com/blog/2015/1/2/creative-crash. Accessed on 5 February 2018.

36. Griffith, E. Why startups fail, according to their founders. *Fortune* (2014). Available at: http://fortune.com/2014/09/25/why-startups-fail-according-to-their-founders/. Accessed on 5 February 2018.

37. Blank, S. Why the lean start-up changes everything. *Harvard Business Review* (2013). Available at: https://hbr.org/2013/05/why-the-lean-start-up-changes-everything. Accessed on 5 February 2018.

38. Griffith, E. Conventional wisdom says 90% of startups fail. Data says otherwise. *Fortune* (2017). Available at: http://fortune.com/2017/06/27/startup-advice-data-failure/. Accessed on 5 February 2018.

39. Cassuto, L. Ph.D. attrition: how much is too much? *The Chronicle of Higher Education* (2013). Available at: http://www.chronicle.com/article/PhD-Attrition-How-Much-Is/140045. Accessed on 5 February 2018.

40. MacLeod, D. Study reveals low PhD completion rates. *The Guardian* (2005). Available at: https://www.theguardian.com/education/2005/jan/11/highereducation.uk1. Accessed on 5 February 2018.

41. Clark, C., Brody, M., Dillon, J., Hart, P. & Heimlich, J. The messy process of research: dilemmas, process, and critique. *Can. J. Environ. Educ.* **12**, 110–126 (2007).

42. Dreamit. Startup loneliness: why it's dangerous and how founders can overcome it. (2016). Available at: https://medium.com/dreamit-perspectives/startup-loneliness-why-its-dangerous-and-how-founders-can-overcome-it-6e85886c588. Accessed on 5 February 2018.

43. Nature Materials. A decade in numbers. *Nat. Mater.* **11**, 743–744 (2012).

44. Hall, T. E. & Steelman, T. A. The development of a discipline: a 20-year evaluation of *Society & Natural Resources. Soc. Nat. Resour.* **20**, 865–881 (2007).

45. nature.com. Editorial criteria and processes. (2017). Available at: http://www.nature.com/nature/authors/get_published/index.html. Accessed on 5 February 2018.

46. Shontell, A. It took Dropbox 7 months to get 1,000,000 users. *Business Insider* (2012). Available at: http://www.businessinsider.com/one-million-users-startups-2012-1?IR=T#it-took-dropbox-7-months-to-get-1000000-users-9. Accessed on 5 February 2018.

47. Shontell, A. Spotify hit its 1,000,000th user 5 months after launch. *Business Insider* (2012). Available at: http://www.businessinsider.com/one-million-users-startups-2012-1?IR=T#spotify-hit-its-1000000th-user-5-months-after-launch-11. Accessed on 5 February 2018.

48. Shontell, A. Instagram was downloaded by 1,000,000 people within 2.5 months. *Business Insider* (2012). Available at: http://www.businessinsider.com/one-million-users-startups-2012-1?IR=T#instagram-was-downloaded-by-1000000-people-within-25-months-12. Accessed on 5 February 2018.

49. http://theleanstartup.com/. Lean startup case studies. (2017). Available at: http://theleanstartup.com/. Accessed on 5 February 2018.

50. Meetup.com. How Instagram used lean startup to build a $1B company. (2012). Available at: https://www.meetup.com/Lean-Startup-Beijing-China/events/64602642/. Accessed on 5 February 2018.

51. Lunden, I. Here's how Spotify scales up and stays agile: it runs 'squads' like lean startups. *techcrunch.com* (2012). Available at: https://techcrunch.com/2012/11/17/heres-how-spotify-scales-up-and-stays-agile-it-runs-squads-like-lean-startups/. Accessed on 5 February 2018.

52. Holliday, L. The strategy udacity uses to scale rapidly. (2016). Available at: https://medium.com/udacity/the-strategy-udacity-uses-to-scale-rapidly-9f5c1086f894. Accessed on 5 February 2018.

53. Ries, E. The lean startup. (2008). Available at: http://www.startuplessonslearned.com/2008/09/lean-startup.html. Accessed on 5 February 2018.

54. Greenwald, T. Upstart Eric Ries has the stage and the crowd is going wild. *Wired* (2012). Available at: https://www.wired.com/2012/05/ff_gururies/all/1. Accessed on 5 February 2018.

55. Roush, W. Eric Ries, the face of the lean startup movement, on how a once-insane idea went mainstream. (2011). Available at: http://www.xconomy.com/san-francisco/2011/07/06/eric-ries-the-face-of-the-lean-startup-movement-on-how-a-once-insane-idea-went-mainstream/. Accessed on 5 February 2018.

56. Blank, S. & Dorf, B. *The Startup Owner's Manual: The Step-By-Step Guide for Building a Great Company.* (K&S Ranch, 2012). Accessed on 5 February 2018.

57. Ferres, Z. Eric Ries on 4 common misconceptions about lean startup. (2017). Available at: https://www.entrepreneur.com/article/286701. Accessed on 5 February 2018.

58. insidehighered.com. Overcoming academic perfectionism. (2012). Available at: https://www.insidehighered.com/career-advice/overcoming-academic-perfectionism. Accessed on 5 February 2018.

59. Rockquemore, K. A. Breaking the cycle. *insidehighered.com* (2012). Available at: https://www.insidehighered.com/advice/2012/11/14/essay-breaking-cycle-academic-perfectionism. Accessed on 5 February 2018.

60. Ayim, A. The MVP you've probably never heard of. *medium.com* (2017). Available at: https://medium.com/ysys/the-mvp-youve-probably-never-heard-of-82a81cc71d3a. Accessed on 5 February 2018.

61. Chawla, D. S. Men cite themselves more than women do. *Nature* **535**, 212 (2016).

62. Vissak, T. How many citations does it take to indicate an academic article is influential? Available at: https://www.researchgate.net/post/How_many_citations_does_it_take_to_indicate_an_academic_article_is_influential. Accessed on 5 February 2018.

63. Flaherty, C. Is retraction the new rebuttal? *insidehighered.com* (2017). Available at: https://www.insidehighered.com/news/2017/09/19/controversy-over-paper-favor-colonialism-sparks-calls-retraction. Accessed on 5 February 2018.

64. Ngo, A. Professors alarmed by blacklist of pro-colonialism author: 'academic thuggery'. *The College Fix* (2017). Available at: https://www.thecollegefix.com/post/37232/. Accessed on 5 February 2018.

65. Flaherty, C. A dangerous withdrawal. *insidehighered.com* (2017). Available at: https://www.insidehighered.com/news/2017/10/09/pro-colonialism-article-has-been-withdrawn-over-threats-journal-editor. Accessed on 5 February 2018.

66. Chubb, J. & Reed, M. 5 ways to fast track the impact of your PhD. *Fast Track Impact* (2017). Available at: http://www.fasttrackimpact.com/single-post/2017/02/08/5-ways-to-fast-track-the-impact-of-your-PhD. Accessed on 5 February 2018.

67. Hower, L. Playing startup. (2015). Available at: http://nextviewventures.com/blog/playing-startup/. Accessed on 5 February 2018.

68. Kim, D. Here's what Yahoo CEO Marissa Mayer said that really made me angry. *yahoo.com* (2016). Available at: https://finance.yahoo.com/news/heres-yahoo-ceo-marissa-mayer-204754971.html. Accessed on 5 February 2018.

69. Matyszczyk, C. Marissa Mayer says the secret of success is working 130 hours a week. (2016). Available at: https://www.cnet.com/au/news/marissa-mayer-says-the-secret-of-success-is-working-130-hours-a-week/. Accessed on 5 February 2018.

70. Ferriss, T. *The 4-Hour Work Week: Escape the 9-5, Live Anywhere and Join the New Rich.* (Random House, 2011).

71. Dore, M. Why you should manage your energy, not your time. *BBC* (2017). Available at: http://www.bbc.com/capital/story/20170612-why-you-should-manage-your-energy-not-your-time. Accessed on 5 February 2018.

72. Schwartz, T. & McCarthy, C. Manage your energy, not your time. *Harvard Business Review* (2007). Available at: https://hbr.org/2007/10/manage-your-energy-not-your-time. Accessed on 5 February 2018.

73. Herrera, T. Work less. You'll get so much more done. *New York Times* (2017). Available at: https://www.nytimes.com/2017/06/26/smarter-living/work-less-youll-get-so-much-more-done.html?mcubz=1. Accessed on 5 February 2018.

74. leanstack.com. 1-page business planning. (2017). Available at: https://leanstack.com/is-one-page-business-model. Accessed on 5 February 2018.

75. Andreessen, M. The PMARCA guide to startups. (2007). Available at: http://pmarchive.com/guide_to_startups_part4.html. Accessed on 5 February 2018.

76. Geissdoerfer, M., Savaget, P., Bocken, N. M. P. & Hultink, E. J. The circular economy – a new sustainability paradigm? *J. Clean. Prod.* **143**, 757–768 (2017).

77. McCartney, M. P., Sullivan, C. & Acreman, M. C. *Ecosystem Impacts of Large Dams.* (Centre for Ecology and Hydrology, 2001).

78. Kirchherr, J. & Charles, K. J. The social impacts of dams: a new framework for scholarly analysis. *Environ. Impact Assess. Rev.* (2016). doi:10.1016/j.eiar.2016.02.005

79. WCD. *Dams and Development – A New Framework for Decision-Making.* (World Commission of Dams, 2000).

80. IHA. *Hydropower Status Report 2016.* (International Hydropower Association, 2016).

81. Krauter, S. ITAIPU. (2015). Available at: http://www.solar.coppe.ufrj.br/itaipu.html.

82. Platts. The top 100 – Part I – The world's largest power plants. (2015). Available at: http://www.industcards.com/top-100-pt-1.htm.

83. Conley, J. P. & Sina Önder, A. The research productivity of new PhDs in economics: the surprisingly high non-success of the successful. *J. Econ. Perspect.* **28**, 205–216 (2014).

84. The Economist. Lazy graduate students? (2014). Available at: https://www. economist.com/blogs/freeexchange/2014/11/productivity-phds. Accessed on 5 February 2018.

85. Warner, J. & Clauset, A. The academy's dirty secret. *slate.com* (2015). Available at: http://www.slate.com/articles/life/education/2015/02/university_hiring_ if_you_didn_t_get_your_ph_d_at_an_elite_university_good.html. Accessed on 5 February 2018.

86. Clauset, A., Arbesman, S. & Larremore, D. B. Systematic inequality and hierarchy in faculty hiring networks. *Sci. Adv.* **1**, (2015).

87. Zarfl, C., Lumsdon, A. E., Berlekamp, J., Tydecks, L. & Tockner, K. A global boom in hydropower dam construction. *Aquat. Sci.* **77**, 161–170 (2015).

88. Kirchherr, J., Charles, K. J. & Walton, M. J. Multi-causal pathways of public opposition to dam projects in Asia: a fuzzy set qualitative comparative analysis (fsQCA). *Glob. Environ. Chang.* **41**, 33–45 (2016).

89. Stark, K. & Stewart, B. What's your unfair advantage? (2012). Available at: https://www.inc.com/karl-and-bill/what-is-your-unfair-advantage.html. Accessed on 5 February 2018.

90. Kirchherr, J. J., Charles, K. & Walton, M. J. The interplay of activists and dam developers: the case of Myanmar's mega-dams. *Int. J. Water Resour. Dev.* **33**, 111–131 (2017).

91. University of Oxford. Guidelines to writing a research proposal (DPhil only). (2017). Available at: http://www.geog.ox.ac.uk/graduate/apply/research_ proposal.html. Accessed on 5 February 2018.

92. Schlenk, C. T. Blackrock investiert in Münchner Scalable Capital. *Gründerszene* (2017). Available at: https://www.gruenderszene.de/allgemein/blackrock-scalable-capital. Accessed on 5 February 2018.

93. Akerlof, G. A. The market for 'lemons': quality uncertainty and the market mechanism. *Q. J. Econ.* **84**, 488–500 (1970).

94. Sharkey, M. 6 things wrong with the 'Lean Startup' model (and what to do about it). (2013). Available at: https://venturebeat.com/2013/10/16/lean-startups-boo/. Accessed on 5 February 2018.

95. Jump, P. PhD: is the doctoral thesis obsolete? *www.timeshighereducation.com* (2015). Available at: https://www.timeshighereducation.com/features/phd-is-the-doctoral-thesis-obsolete/2020255.article#survey-answer. Accessed on 5 February 2018.

96. Cowton, C. Looks good on paper... *timeshighereducation.com* (2011). Available at: https://www.timeshighereducation.com/features/looks-good-on-paper/416988.article. Accessed on 5 February 2018.

97. Goethe University Frankfurt. Frequently asked questions about publication-based ('cumulative') dissertations in English. (2017). Available at: https://www. uni-frankfurt.de/40165835/CumulativeDissertationsenglish.pdf. Accessed on 5 February 2018.

98. Advanced Materials. Guide for authors. (2017). Available at: http://onlinelibrary.wiley.com/store/10.1002/(ISSN)1521-4095/asset/homepages/2089_guidelines.pdf?v=1&s=43552fa607cff2d2ce59eac13494c0a005bf9ad6&isAguDoi=false.
99. Universität Salzburg. Abschlussarbeiten. (2017). Available at: https://www.uni-salzburg.at/index.php?id=202621. Accessed on 5 February 2018.
100. The past, present and future of the PhD thesis. *Nature* **535**, 7 (2016).
101. Biswas, A. K. & Kirchherr, J. Prof, no one is reading you. *The Straits Times* (2015). Available at: http://www.straitstimes.com/opinion/prof-no-one-is-reading-you. Accessed on 5 February 2018.
102. Remler, D. Are 90% of academic papers really never cited? Reviewing the literature on academic citations. *LSE IMPACT Blog* (2014). Available at: http://blogs.lse.ac.uk/impactofsocialsciences/2014/04/23/academic-papers-citation-rates-remler/. Accessed on 5 February 2018.
103. University of Warwick. Six misconceptions about the three-paper route. (2017). Available at: https://phdlife.warwick.ac.uk/2017/04/19/six-misconceptions-about-three-paper-route/. Accessed on 5 February 2018.
104. Waters, T. When is peer review the gold standard, and when is it only tin? (2016). Available at: http://www.ethnography.com/2016/10/when-is-peer-review-the-gold-standard-and-when-is-it-only-tin/. Accessed on 5 February 2018.
105. Przem. Will using lean startup allow you to cut costs? (2017). Available at: https://www.growly.io/will-using-lean-startup-allow-you-to-cut-costs/. Accessed on 5 February 2018.
106. Kickstarter. Home. (2017). Available at: https://www.kickstarter.com/. Accessed on 5 February 2018.
107. GoFundMe. Home. (2017). Available at: https://de.gofundme.com/. Accessed on 5 February 2018.
108. Harvilicz, D. The democratizing power of crowdfunding and the JOBS Act. *Huffington Post* (2014). Available at: http://www.huffingtonpost.com/dave-harvilicz/the-democratizing-power-o_b_5162659.html. Accessed on 5 February 2018.
109. Gaskell, A. The rise of investment crowdfunding. *Forbes* (2016). Available at: https://www.forbes.com/sites/adigaskell/2016/03/15/the-rise-of-investment-crowdfunding/#488a1f184d9b. Accessed on 5 February 2018.
110. World Bank. Crowdfunding's potential for the developing world. (2013). Available at: http://www.infodev.org/infodev-files/wb_crowdfundingreport-v12.pdf. Accessed on 5 February 2018.
111. Goldman Sachs. *The Future of Finance: The Socialization of Finance.* (2015).
112. Watson, E. A. Fund my DPhil at Oxford University! (2015). Available at: https://www.gofundme.com/fund-my-phd-eleri. Accessed on 5 February 2018.

113. Sandlund, J. Crowdfunding motivations — what drives people to invest? (2013). Available at: http://www.thecrowdcafe.com/crowdfunding-motivations/. Accessed on 5 February 2018.

114. Studienstiftung des deutschen Volkes. Offene Stipendienprogramme / McCloy. (2017). Available at: https://www.studienstiftung.de/mccloy/. Accessed on 5 February 2018.

115. Finneran, J. The fat startup: learn the lessons of my failed lean startup. (2013). Available at: http://www.johnffinneran.com/blog/fat-startup-learn-the-lessons. Accessed on 5 February 2018.

116. Oakes, K. 25 brutally honest peer review comments from scientists. *BuzzFeed* (2014). Available at: https://www.buzzfeed.com/kellyoakes/more-like-smear-review-amirite?utm_term=.eoeAEA6dWV#.kaKYzYkrBo. Accessed on 5 February 2018.

117. Kahneman, D. & Lovallo, D. Timid choices and bold forecasts: a cognitive perspective on risk taking. *Manage. Sci.* **39**, 17–31 (1993).

118. Bornmann, L., Mutz, R., Daniel, H.-D., Berlin, J. & Waeckerle, J. A reliability-generalization study of journal peer reviews: a multilevel meta-analysis of inter-rater reliability and its determinants. *PLoS One* **5**, e14331 (2010).

119. Vines, T. Is peer review a coin toss? (2011). Available at: https://scholarly kitchen.sspnet.org/2011/12/08/is-peer-review-a-coin-toss/. Accessed on 5 February 2018.

120. Kirchherr, J., Matthews, N., Charles, K. J. & Walton, M. J. 'Learning it the hard way': social safeguards norms in Chinese-led dam projects in Myanmar, Laos and Cambodia. *Energy Policy* **102**, 529–539 (2017).

121. Tunkelang, D. Least publishable unit. (2009). Available at: http://thenoisy channel.com/2009/03/16/least-publishable-unit. Accessed on 5 February 2018.

122. The cost of salami slicing. *Nat. Mater.* **4**, 1 (2005).

123. Seglen, P. O. The skewness of science. *J. Am. Soc. Inf. Sci.* **43**, 628–638 (1992).

124. Vanclay, J. K. Impact factor: outdated artefact or stepping-stone to journal certification? (2012). doi:10.1007/s11192-011-0561-0

125. Greene, S. The role of task in the development of academic thinking through reading and writing in a college history course. *Research in the Teaching of English* **27**, 46–75 (1993).

126. Greene, S. Mining texts in reading to write. *J. Adv Compos.* **12**, 151–170 (1992).

127. Flower, L. The construction of purpose in writing and reading. *Coll. English* **50**, 528–550 (1988).

128. Stotsky, S. Research on reading/writing relationships: a synthesis and suggested directions. *Lang. Arts* **60**, 627–642 (1983).

129. Dunleavy, P. How to write paragraphs in research texts (articles, books and PhDs). (2014). Available at: https://medium.com/advice-and-help-in-authoring-a-phd-or-non-fiction/how-to-write-paragraphs-80781e2f3054. Accessed on 5 February 2018.

130. Silverman, L. K. *Upside-Down Brilliance: The Visual-Spatial Learner.* (DeLeon Publishing, 2005).

131. Goins, J. How to overcome writer's block: 14 tricks that work. (2017). Available at: https://goinswriter.com/how-to-overcome-writers-block/. Accessed on 5 February 2018.

132. tckpublishing.com. 5 ways writing by hand can boost your creative career. (2017). Available at: https://www.tckpublishing.com/5-reasons-to-write-by-hand/. Accessed on 5 February 2018.

133. Taber, M. The single founder myth. (2006). Available at: http://www.singlefounder.com/thesinglefoundermyth/. Accessed on 5 February 2018.

134. Graham, P. The 18 mistakes that kill startups. (2006). Available at: http://www.paulgraham.com/startupmistakes.html. Accessed on 5 February 2018.

135. Kamps, H. J. Breaking a myth: data shows you don't actually need a co-founder. (2016). Available at: https://techcrunch.com/2016/08/26/co-founders-optional/. Accessed on 5 February 2018.

136. Mansfield, M. Startup statistics – the numbers you need to know. (2016). Available at: https://smallbiztrends.com/2016/11/startup-statistics-small-business.html. Accessed on 5 February 2018.

137. Bastian, H. Science and the rise of the co-authors. (2015). Available at: http://blogs.plos.org/absolutely-maybe/2015/11/25/science-and-the-rise-of-the-co-authors/. Accessed on 5 February 2018.

138. Beaver, D. deB & Rosen, R. Studies in scientific collaboration Part III. Professionalization and the natural history of modern scientific co-authorship. *Scientometrics* **1**, 231–245 (1979).

139. Weeks, W. B., Wallace, A. E. & Kimberly, B. C. S. Changes in authorship patterns in prestigious US medical journals. *Soc. Sci. Med.* **59**, 1949–1954 (2004).

140. Ossenblok, T. L. B., Verleysen, F. T. & Engels, T. C. E. Coauthorship of journal articles and book chapters in the social sciences and humanities (2000–2010). *J. Assoc. Inf. Sci. Technol.* **65**, 882–897 (2014).

141. Grove, J. Is mass authorship destroying the credibility of papers? (2015). Available at: https://www.timeshighereducation.com/news/mass-authorship-destroying-credibility-papers. Accessed on 5 February 2018.

142. Faulkes, Z. When does authorship stop meaning anything useful? (2015). Available at: http://neurodojo.blogspot.de/2015/05/when-does-authorship-stop-meaning.html. Accessed on 5 February 2018.

143. Castelvecchi, D. Physics paper sets record with more than 5,000 authors. *Nature* (2015). doi:10.1038/nature.2015.17567

144. Atkinson, R. & Flint, J. *Accessing Hidden and Hard-to-Reach Populations: Snowball Research Strategies.* (University of Surrey, 2001).

145. Piper, A. & Wellmon, C. Publication, power, and patronage: on inequality and academic publishing. (2017). doi:10.6084/M9.FIGSHARE.4558072.V2

146. Flaherty, C. Publishing's prestige bias. (2017). Available at: https://www. insidehighered.com/news/2017/01/20/study-suggests-top-humanities-journals-favor-research-elite-institutions. Accessed on 5 February 2018.

147. Kirchherr, J., Disselhoff, T. & Charles, K. Safeguards, financing, and employment in Chinese infrastructure projects in Africa: the case of Ghana's Bui Dam. *Waterlines* **35**, 37–58 (2016).

148. Arnold, W. What role do agile/scrum play in the lean startup? (2015). Available at: https://www.quora.com/What-role-do-agile-scrum-play-in-the-lean-startup. Accessed on 5 February 2018.

149. Sutherland, J. & Schwaber, K. What is scrum? (2017). Available at: http://www.scrumguides.org/. Accessed on 5 February 2018.

150. Novick, G. Is there a bias against telephone interviews in qualitative research? *Res. Nurs. Health* **31**, 391–398 (2008).

151. Reich, W. & Earls, F. Interviewing adolescents by telephone: is it a useful methodological strategy? *Compr. Psychiatry* **31**, 211–215 (1990).

152. Hanna, P. Using internet technologies (such as Skype) as a research medium: a research note. *Qual. Res.* **12**, 239–242 (2012).

153. Ohr, T. Pitch your startup at the EU-Startups Conference 2017 in Berlin. (2017). Available at: http://www.eu-startups.com/2017/01/pitch-your-startup-at-the-eu-startups-conference-2017/. Accessed on 5 February 2018.

154. ACL. Conference acceptance rates. (2017). Available at: https://aclweb.org/aclwiki/Conference_acceptance_rates. Accessed on 5 February 2018.

155. Taplin, J. Anonymity brings out the worst in humans. *TIME* (2015). Available at: http://time.com/collection-post/4028444/jonathan-taplin-should-we-let-ourselves-be-anonymous-online/. Accessed on 5 February 2018.

156. Kirchherr, J. & Biswas, A. K. Expensive academic conferences give us old ideas and no new faces. *The Guardian* (2017). Available at: https://www.theguardian.com/higher-education-network/2017/aug/30/expensive-academic-conferences-give-us-old-ideas-and-no-new-faces. Accessed on 5 February 2018.

157. Nazar, J. 14 famous business pivots. *Forbes* (2013). Available at: https://www.forbes.com/sites/jasonnazar/2013/10/08/14-famous-business-pivots/#42065ba25797. Accessed on 5 February 2018.

158. Fiegerman, S. Twitter is now losing users in the U.S. (2017). Available at: http://money.cnn.com/2017/07/27/technology/business/twitter-earnings/index.html.

159. BBC. Starbucks reports record annual profit. (2016). Available at: http://www.bbc.com/news/business-37868620. Accessed on 5 February 2018.

160. University of Oxford. Key milestones for DPhil students. (2017). Available at: https://www.ox.ac.uk/students/academic/guidance/graduate/research/status/DPhil?wssl=1. Accessed on 5 February 2018.

161. Yoskovitz, B. What's the motivation to start a startup? *Instigator Blog* (2007). Available at: http://www.instigatorblog.com/whats-the-motivation-to-start-a-startup/2007/07/03/. Accessed on 5 February 2018.

162. Shah, D. 12 facts about entrepreneurs that will likely surprise you. (2009). Available at: http://onstartups.com/tabid/3339/bid/10561/12-Facts-About-Entrepreneurs-That-Will-Likely-Surprise-You.aspx. Accessed on 5 February 2018.

163. Drake, D. 6 startup exit strategies for investors. *Huffington Post* (2016). Available at: http://www.huffingtonpost.com/david-drake/six-startup-exit-strategies_b_8254780.html. Accessed on 5 February 2018.

164. Kosoff, M. These 20 VC-backed companies had the biggest exits of the last year. *Business Insider* (2015). Available at: http://www.businessinsider.com/the-20-biggest-vc-backed-company-exits-of-2015-2016-1?international=true&r=US&IR=T/#3-cardioxyl-pharmaceuticals-sold-for-207-billion-18. Accessed on 5 February 2018.

165. Pepitone, J. #WOW! Twitter soars 73% in IPO. *CNN* (2013). Available at: http://money.cnn.com/2013/11/07/technology/social/twitter-ipo-stock/index.html. Accessed on 5 February 2018.

166. Judson, B. How to make Twitter profitable. *techcrunch.com* (2017). Available at: https://techcrunch.com/2017/04/22/how-to-make-twitter-profitable/. Accessed on 5 February 2018.

167. Edwards, J. Twitter's IPO will make all these people millionaires and billionaires. *Business Insider* (2013). Available at: http://www.businessinsider.com/twitters-ipo-will-make-all-these-people-millionaires-2013-10?international=true&r=US&IR=T#. Accessed on 5 February 2018.

168. Goldman, D. 10 years later, Twitter still isn't close to making money. *CNN* (2016). Available at: http://money.cnn.com/2016/03/21/technology/twitter-10th-anniversary/index.html. Accessed on 5 February 2018.

169. Thomas, K. Finishing your PhD thesis: 15 top tips from those in the know. *The Guardian* (2014). Available at: https://www.theguardian.com/higher-education-network/blog/2014/aug/27/finishing-phd-thesis-top-tips-experts-advice. Accessed on 5 February 2018.

170. Ransan-Cooper, H. Does my PhD have to save the world? *The Thesis Whisperer* (2013). Available at: https://thesiswhisperer.com/2013/07/24/do-you-have-to-save-the-world/. Accessed on 5 February 2018.

171. Schonlau, M. How to finish a Ph.D. (2003). Available at: http://www.schonlau.net/finishphd.html. Accessed on 5 February 2018.

172. Sachs, J. Factor costs and macroeconomic adjustment in the open economy: theory and evidence. PhD dissertation. (Harvard University, 1980).

173. Google Scholar. Jeffrey Sachs. (2017). Available at: https://scholar.google.com/citations?hl=en&user=u5I3DeMAAAAJ&view_op=list_works&sortby=pubdate. Accessed on 5 February 2018.

174. Sachs, J. Full Bio. (2017). Available at: http://jeffsachs.org/about/. Accessed on 5 February 2018.

175. Green, E. What are the most-cited publications in the social sciences (according to Google Scholar)? *LSE IMPACT Blog* (2016). Available at: http://blogs. lse.ac.uk/impactofsocialsciences/2016/05/12/what-are-the-most-cited-publications-in-the-social-sciences-according-to-google-scholar/. Accessed on 5 February 2018.

176. Maxwell, V. The vicious triangle of perfectionism, anxiety & depression. *Psychology Today* (2012). Available at: https://www.psychologytoday.com/blog/crazy-life/201201/the-vicious-triangle-perfectionism-anxiety-depression. Accessed on 5 February 2018.

177. Smith, A. W. Why being a perfectionist can make you depressed. *Everyday Health* (2013). Available at: https://www.everydayhealth.com/depression/being-a-perfectionist-can-make-you-depressed.aspx. Accessed on 5 February 2018.

178. O'Connor, R. C., Rasmussen, S. & Hawton, K. Predicting depression, anxiety and self-harm in adolescents: the role of perfectionism and acute life stress. *Behav. Res. Ther.* **48**, 52–59 (2010).

179. Räth, G. Math 42 nach dem 20-Millionen-Exit: "Solche Summen fühlen sich sehr merkwürdig an". *Gründerszene* (2017). Available at: https://www.gruenderszene.de/allgemein/math-42-exit-interview-maxim-nitsche. Accessed on 5 February 2018.

180. The Wall Street Journal. Your startup gets bought. What next? (2015). Available at: https://www.wsj.com/articles/your-startup-gets-bought-what-next-1432317743. Accessed on 5 February 2018.

181. Rao, L. GrandCentral to (finally) launch as Google Voice. It's very, very good. *techcrunch.com* (2009). Available at: https://techcrunch.com/2009/03/11/grand-central-to-finally-launch-as-google-voice-its-very-very-good/. Accessed on 5 February 2018.

182. Schroter, S. *et al.* What errors do peer reviewers detect, and does training improve their ability to detect them? *J. R. Soc. Med.* **101**, 507–514 (2008).

183. Lindner, M. Their Work Weeks. *Forbes* (2009). Available at: https://www.forbes.com/2009/09/08/work-hours-ten-questions-entrepreneurs-promising.html. Accessed on 5 February 2018.

184. Rees, E. *The Slow Professor: Challenging the Culture of Speed in the Academy*, by Maggie Berg and Barbara K. Seeber. (2016). Available at: https://www.timeshighereducation.com/books/review-the-slow-professor-maggie-berg-barbara-seeber-university-of-toronto-press. Accessed on 5 February 2018.

185. Berg, M. & Seeber, B. *The Slow Professor: Challenging the Culture of Speed in the Academy.* (University of Toronto Press, 2016).

186. Flaherty, C. 'The Slow Professor'. (2016). Available at: https://www.insidehighered.com/news/2016/04/19/book-argues-faculty-members-should-actively-resist-culture-speed-modern-academe. Accessed on 5 February 2018.

187. Best, D. J. *A Professor at the End of Time: The Work and Future of the Professoriate*. (Rutgers University Press, 2017).

188. Enright, M. The Slow Professor movement: reclaiming the intellectual life of the university. (2017). Available at: http://www.cbc.ca/radio/thesunday edition/flynngate-watergate-stiglitz-on-world-economy-stuart-mclean-s-documentaries-slow-professor-movement-1.3985655/the-slow-professor-movement-reclaiming-the-intellectual-life-of-the-university-1.3985671. Accessed on 5 February 2018.

189. Mason, M. Sample size and saturation in PhD studies using qualitative interviews. *Forum Qualitative Sozialforschung/Forum: Qual. Soc. Res.* **11** (2010). Available at: http://www.qualitative-research.net/index.php/fqs/article/view/1428/3027. Accessed on 6 March 2018.

190. University of Oxford. DPhil handbook. (2016). Available at: https://weblearn.ox.ac.uk/access/lessonbuilder/item/99075/group/9691ebb2-1e41-45aa-b280-db8b45bc3d91/lessons/Graduate Course Handbooks/DPhil Handbook 2016 v1.0 20092016.pdf.

191. Baron, R. M. & Kenny, D. A. The moderator-mediator variable distinction in social psychological research: conceptual, strategic, and statistical considerations. *J. Pers. Soc. Psychol.* **51**, 1173–1182 (1986).

192. Biswas, A. K. & Kirchherr, J. The tough life of an academic entrepreneur: innovative commercial and non-commercial ventures must be encouraged. *LSE IMPACT Blog* (2016). Available at: http://blogs.lse.ac.uk/impactofsocialsciences/2016/02/16/the-tough-life-of-an-academic-entrepreneur/. Accessed on 5 February 2018.

193. Kirchherr, J. Why we can't trust academic journals to tell the scientific truth. *The Guardian* (2017). Available at: https://www.theguardian.com/higher-education-network/2017/jun/06/why-we-cant-trust-academic-journals-to-tell-the-scientific-truth. Accessed on 5 February 2018.

194. Kirchherr, J. & Walton, M. The NLD should start 2017 by scrapping the Myitsone dam. *Myanmar Times* (2017). Available at: http://www.mmtimes.com/index.php/opinion/24387-the-nld-should-start-2017-by-scrapping-the-myitsone-dam.html. Accessed on 5 February 2018.

195. Ramsey, A. Is it too late to save Myanmar's threatened ecosystems? *OZY Magazine* (2017). Available at: http://www.ozy.com/fast-forward/is-it-too-late-to-save-myanmars-threatened-ecosystems/75767. Accessed on 5 February 2018.

196. Higgins, A. & Klein, S. in *Accelerating Global Supply Chains with IT-Innovation* 31–36 (Springer Berlin Heidelberg, 2011). doi:10.1007/978-3-642-15669-4_2

197. Tugend, A. Winners never quit? Well, yes, they do. *New York Times* (2008). Available at: http://www.nytimes.com/2008/08/16/business/16shortcuts.html. Accessed on 5 February 2018.

198. Brown, D. Here's what 'fail fast' really means. *Venture Beat* (2015). Available at: https://venturebeat.com/2015/03/15/heres-what-fail-fast-really-means/. Accessed on 5 February 2018.

199. Patel, N. 90% of startups fail: here's what you need to know about the 10%. *Forbes* (2015). Available at: https://www.forbes.com/sites/neilpatel/2015/01/16/90-of-startups-will-fail-heres-what-you-need-to-know-about-the-10/#392985386679. Accessed on 5 February 2018.

200. Gleeson, B. 7 reasons why 90% of start-ups fail and how to be the 10%. *Inc.* (2016). Available at: https://www.inc.com/brent-gleeson/7-reasons-why-90-of-start-ups-fail-and-how-to-be-the-10.html. Accessed on 5 February 2018.

201. Dunn, S. In hindsight: former Ph.D. students reflect on why they jumped ship. *Chronicle Vitae* (2014). Available at: https://chroniclevitae.com/news/445-in-hindsight-former-ph-d-students-reflect-on-why-they-jumped-ship. Accessed on 5 February 2018.

202. Peironcely, J. The PhD dilemma: should you quit your PhD or stay? *Next Scientist* (2014). Available at: http://www.nextscientist.com/phd-dilemma-quit-your-phd/. Accessed on 5 February 2018.

203. Haushofer, J. Johannes Haushofer – CV of failures. Available at: https://www.princeton.edu/~joha/Johannes_Haushofer_CV_of_Failures.pdf. Accessed on 5 February 2018.

204. Stefan, M. A CV of failures. *Nature* **468**, 467–467 (2010).

205. Hushna, S. What would happen without science? (2015). Available at: http://sciencetheworks.blogspot.com.cy/2015/09/what-would-happen-without-science.html. Accessed on 5 February 2018.

206. World Bank. Life expectancy at birth, total (years). Available at: https://data.worldbank.org/indicator/SP.DYN.LE00.IN. Accessed on 6 March 2018.

207. Maidment, P. Elon Musk/Stanford. (2016). Available at: https://www.cnbc.com/2014/11/03/college-dropouts-who-made-millions.html#slide=3. Accessed on 5 February 2018.

208. BrainyQuote. Elon Musk quotes. (2017). Available at: https://www.brainyquote.com/quotes/quotes/e/elonmusk567259.html. Accessed on 5 February 2018.

209. Kobayter, S. Doing vs. thinking: valuable PhD transferable skills. *Huffington Post* (2014). Available at: http://www.huffingtonpost.com/sabine-kobayter-/identifying-those-valuabl_b_5542058.html. Accessed on 5 February 2018.

210. Patterson, E. Why do so many graduate students quit? *The Atlantic* (2016). Available at: https://www.theatlantic.com/education/archive/2016/07/why-do-so-many-graduate-students-quit/490094/. Accessed on 5 February 2018.

211. The Economist. The disposable academic. (2010). Available at: http://www.economist.com/node/17723223. Accessed on 5 February 2018.

212. Nyquist, J. & Woodford, B. *Re-Envisioning the PhD: What Concerns Do We Have?* (Australian National University, 2000).

213. Kahn, S. & Ginther, D. K. The impact of postdoctoral training on early careers in biomedicine. *Nat. Biotechnol.* **35**, 90–94 (2017).

214. Powell, D. The price of doing a postdoc. *Science (80-.).* (2017). doi:10.1126/science.caredit.a1700003

215. Kuo, M. What comes after a Ph.D.? Check out the data. *Science (80-.).* (2017).

216. Business Insider Nederland. Waarom de meeste Amerikaanse miljonairs niet uitblinken op de middelbare school. *Business Insider* (2017). Available at: https://www.businessinsider.nl/eric-barker-millionaires-bad-grades-gpa-2017-6/?international=true&r=US. Accessed on 5 February 2018.

217. Lindsay, S. What's the average college GPA? By major? *PrepScholar* (2015). Available at: https://blog.prepscholar.com/average-college-gpa-by-major. Accessed on 5 February 2018.

218. Weissman, J. How many Ph.D.'s actually get to become college professors? *The Atlantic* (2013). Available at: https://www.theatlantic.com/business/archive/2013/02/how-many-phds-actually-get-to-become-college-professors/273434/. Accessed on 5 February 2018.

219. Nerad, M., Aanerud, R. & Cerny, J. in *Paths to the Professoriate: Strategies for Enriching the Preparation of Future Faculty* (Wiley, 1999).

220. Wolff, J. Doctor, doctor ... we're suffering a glut of PhDs who can't find academic jobs. *The Guardian* (2015). Available at: https://www.theguardian.com/education/2015/apr/21/phd-cant-find-academic-job-university. Accessed on 5 February 2018.

221. Weissman, J. The ever-shrinking role of tenured college professors (in 1 chart). *The Atlantic* (2013). Available at: https://www.theatlantic.com/business/archive/2013/04/the-ever-shrinking-role-of-tenured-college-professors-in-1-chart/274849/. Accessed on 5 February 2018.

222. Patton, S. The Ph.D. now comes with food stamps. *The Chronicle of Higher Education* (2012). Available at: http://www.chronicle.com/article/From-Graduate-School-to/131795/. Accessed on 5 February 2018.

223. Gee, A. Facing poverty, academics turn to sex work and sleeping in cars. *The Guardian* (2017). Available at: https://www.theguardian.com/us-news/2017/sep/28/adjunct-professors-homeless-sex-work-academia-poverty. Accessed on 5 February 2018.

224. Caplan, S. Running science as a Ponzi scheme. *The Guardian* (2012). Available at: https://www.theguardian.com/science/occams-corner/2012/nov/23/running-science-ponzi-scheme. Accessed on 5 February 2018.

225. Afonso, A. How academia resembles a drug gang. *LSE IMPACT Blog* (2013). Available at: http://blogs.lse.ac.uk/impactofsocialsciences/2013/12/11/how-academia-resembles-a-drug-gang/. Accessed on 5 February 2018.

226. McLaughlin, J. 21st century science: an academic pyramid scheme? *Scizzle Blog* (2015). Available at: http://www.myscizzle.com/blog/21st-century-science-an-academic-pyramid-scheme/. Accessed on 5 February 2018.

227. The Economist. *Why doing a PhD is often a waste of time.* (2016). Available at: https://medium.economist.com/why-doing-a-phd-is-often-a-waste-of-time-349206f9addb. Accessed on 6 March 2018.

228. Croucher, G. It's time to reduce the number of PhD students, or rethink how doctoral programs work. *The Conversation* (2016). Available at: https://theconversation.com/its-time-to-reduce-the-number-of-phd-students-or-rethink-how-doctoral-programs-work-68972. Accessed on 5 February 2018.

229. Tucker, J. A. Academe as meritocracy. *insidehighered.com* (2011). Available at: https://www.insidehighered.com/advice/2011/01/31/another_view_on_graduate_programs_and_the_academic_job_market. Accessed on 5 February 2018.

230. Afonso, A. Academic labour markets in Europe vary widely in openness and job security. *LSE IMPACT Blog* (2017). Available at: http://blogs.lse.ac.uk/impactofsocialsciences/2016/11/21/academic-labour-markets-in-europe-vary-widely-in-openness-and-job-security/. Accessed on 5 February 2018.

231. Bartoloni, M. La cattedra non è per giovani: solo 36 professori in Italia hanno meno di 40 anni. *Scuola24* (2016). Available at: http://www.scuola24.ilsole24ore.com/art/universita-e-ricerca/2016-11-03/la-cattedra-non-e-giovani-solo-36-professori-ordinari-italia-hanno-meno-40-anni-181909.php?uuid=ADPwQuoB&refresh_ce=1. Accessed on 5 February 2018.

232. Warodell, J., Olsson, E. J. & Almäng, J. Swedish academia is no meritocracy. *timeshighereducation.com* (2017). Available at: https://www.timeshighereducation.com/opinion/swedish-academia-is-no-meritocracy. Accessed on 5 February 2018.

233. Afonso, A. Varieties of academic labor markets in Europe. *PS Polit. Sci. Polit.* **49**, 816–821 (2016).

234. Greenhalgh, L. Commission to reject more applicants at first hurdle. *European Commission* (2016). Available at: http://www.researchresearch.com/news/article/?articleId=1357206. Accessed on 5 February 2018.

235. Volkswagen Stiftung. Challenges for Europe. (2017). Available at: https://www.volkswagenstiftung.de/en/funding/our-funding-portfolio-at-a-glance/challenges-for-europe.html. Accessed on 5 February 2018.

236. Rees, J. Get your manuscript out! *Chronicle Vitae* (2016). Available at: https://chroniclevitae.com/news/1492-get-your-manuscript-out. Accessed on 5 February 2018.

237. Dahlsrud, A. How corporate social responsibility is defined: an analysis of 37 definitions. *Corp. Soc. Responsib. Environ. Manag.* **15**, 1–13 (2008).

238. Kirchherr, J., Reike, D. & Hekkert, M. Conceptualizing the circular economy: an analysis of 114 definitions. *Resour. Conserv. Recycl.* **127**, 221–232 (2017).

239. Lieder, M. & Rashid, A. Towards circular economy implementation: a comprehensive review in context of manufacturing industry. *J. Clean. Prod.* **115**, 36–51 (2016).

240. Altmetric. Altmetrics can showcase the attention and influence of research. (2017). Available at: https://www.altmetric.com/about-altmetrics/what-are-altmetrics/. Accessed on 5 February 2018.

241. REACH. About REACH. (2017). Available at: http://reachwater.org.uk/about-reach/. Accessed on 5 February 2018.

242. Bajpai, K. Facebook. (2017). Available at: https://www.facebook.com/nuslkyspp/photos/rpp.119629194743652/1621466531226570/?type=3 &theater.

243. Colao, J. Steve Blank introduces scientists to a new variable: customers. *Forbes* (2012). Available at: https://www.forbes.com/sites/jjcolao/2012/08/01/steve-blank-introduces-scientists-to-a-new-variable-customers/#2e9c47a359b4. Accessed on 5 February 2018.

Index